Praise for *Emotional Intelligence for Religious Leaders*

"As I finished reading *Emotional Intelligence for Religious Leaders*, my first thought was how valuable this would have been more than twenty years ago when I started ministry. I was equipped with biblical knowledge, but I was clueless of the internal demands and stresses of ministry. My degrees were beneficial, but all three were sorely lacking in the area of emotional intelligence."
—Barry Park, senior minister, University Christian Church

"For decades, we have mistakenly downplayed the importance of pastoral leadership. And yet, congregations succeed or fail in their mission, oftentimes, in direct relation to the effectiveness of their pastors. *Emotional Intelligence for Religious Leaders* recognizes not only the importance of pastoral leadership but emotionally intelligent and healthy pastoral leadership. It is a must-read for any pastor seeking to maximize her or his potential as a spiritual leader."
—John Wimberly, congregational consultant

"C. S. Lewis said, in reference to his writings, 'Until the theologians and the ordained clergy begin to communicate with ordinary people in the vernacular, in a way that they can understand, I'm going to have to do this sort of thing.'

"Thanks to libraries, bookstores, and websites we have Lewis. Thanks to John West and his fellow writers, whom I strongly suspect already see through the wry scholar's eyes, there is added hope for our generations of clergy and lay professionals. *Emotional Intelligence for Religious Leaders* offers no less than collaborative brilliance. It serves up fresh insight and access to tools already at work in the helping sciences.

"Some in the clergy cringe at the mere mention of psychology. They shouldn't. The word originates in the Greek, and 'psych' translates as 'soul' and suffix 'logy' or 'logos' translates as premise, discourse, or opinion. 'Discourse of the soul' is shared territory for pastors and psychologists alike. It's the same turf.

"Clergy moves in these arenas just as ably as the behavioralists. Perhaps even more so, for a fire burns in the souls of pastors and lay leaders alike, a fire unrestrained by limits of reason, hypothesis, or the scientific method.

"Clergy should know that wisdoms lay on the other side, answers that address the ordinary, irksome issues that confront faith professionals almost daily. The writers share their own stories. They share how added skills in communication, sensitivity, and emotional intelligence worked for them; how they've shed administrative weights. They've separated the wheat from the chaff for us, and, in doing so, served the readers with a rich menu of ideas. They offer an approachable, understandable frame of reference that serves the cause of our faith without undermining any of the orthodoxy in its mission. Please, check it out."

—Mark Sellers, founder, New Covenant Soul Care

"When I read the title of one section, 'Religious Organizations Are Not Families,' I was instantly sold on this book. It is a much-needed resource at a time when emotional intelligence is crucial to the success of any leader and any congregation."

—Greg Rickel, Bishop of the Diocese of Olympia

"'If you will not take too much time, I will wait for you the rest of my life.' Every year or so, something comes along that I feel I have been waiting for for a long, long while. This describes perfectly the impact on me of *Emotional Intelligence for Religious Leaders* by John Lee West, Roy M. Oswald, and Nadyne Guzmán. These three authors, through their intellect, their honesty and openness about their own journeys, and clarity of presentation have provided a personal 'GPS' for all who want to understand and move toward effective and human leadership within any and all religious systems.

"By focusing on six basic traits within the EQ Model, they have created a roadmap to Emotional Intelligence that is both manageable and usable.

"No longer can anyone say, 'If only I had known about this earlier in my career.' As the Chinese proverb says: 'The best time to plant a tree was twenty years ago.' The second-best time is NOW!"

—C. Waite Maclin, chair, Center for Emotional Intelligence and Human Relations Training

"One only needs to read the highlights of the latest religious news to know the tremendous importance for just not religious leaders but boards and leadership teams of religious groups to understand, learn, and apply the information in this wonderful book on Emotional Intelligence (EQ). From the Catholic Church's relatively recent focus on affective maturity in the formation of priests to the burnout of Protestant megachurch leaders, the clear message is right dogma, proclamation skills, and business acumen are not enough. EQ is also required for not only effective but sustainable ministry. The book's layout of progressive steps in developing EQ will be an excellent journey for those who have the courage to truly look behind the 'false self' to develop their EQ for leadership, and as noted in chapter 9, to see how deeply these steps tie into one's own spirituality. I heard the ring of truth throughout this book and realized part of this ringing is from knowing and working with one of the authors, Dr. John West. His life is one of authentic EQ in his life and work with others."

—Harvey Payne, Divine Mercy University

"As a faith leader pastoring a congregation, I cannot think of more important work than what is offered by West, Oswald, and Guzmán. This book's ability to articulate what Emotional Intelligence is while also providing a framework for engaging and strengthening one's own Emotional Intelligence (EQ) should be required reading for all religious leaders, lay and clergy."

—Corbin Tobey-Davis, Parkview Congregational Church
UCC

EMOTIONAL INTELLIGENCE FOR RELIGIOUS LEADERS

John Lee West, Roy M. Oswald, and Nadyne Guzmán

An Alban Institute Book

ROWMAN & LITTLEFIELD
Lanham • Boulder • New York • London

Published by Rowman & Littlefield
An imprint of The Rowman & Littlefield Publishing Group, Inc.
4501 Forbes Boulevard, Suite 200, Lanham, Maryland 20706
https://rowman.com

Unit A, Whitacre Mews, 26-34 Stannary Street, London SE11 4AB, United Kingdom

British Library Cataloguing in Publication Information Available

Library of Congress Cataloging-in-Publication Data
Names: West, John Lee, author.
Title: Emotional intelligence for religious leaders / John Lee West, Roy M.
    Oswald, and Nadyne Guzm?an.
Description: Lanham : Alban Books-Rowman & Littlefield, 2018. | "An Alban
    Institute book." | Includes bibliographical references and index.
Identifiers: LCCN 2018014153 (print) | LCCN 2018021049 (ebook) | ISBN
    9781538109151 (ebook) | ISBN 9781538109137 (hardback : alk. paper) |
    ISBN 9781538109144 (pbk. : alk. paper)
Subjects: LCSH: Leadership—Religious aspects. | Religious leaders. | Emo-
    tional intelligence. | Psychology, Religious.
Classification: LCC BL65.L42 (ebook) | LCC BL65.L42 W47 2018 (print) |
    DDC 152.402/42—dc23
LC record available at https://lccn.loc.gov/2018014153

Printed in the United States of America

CONTENTS

PREFACE

The three of us came together to share our thoughts, ideas, and experiences about Emotional Intelligence (EQ) and its importance in the lives of religious leaders. Through our collective experiences and research, we discovered that EQ is essential for religious leadership, and it is foundational for developing and maintaining successful relationships. We also found that expanding EQ can positively affect the emotional maturity and spiritual depth of religious leaders.

Each of us came to this project from a different, yet parallel set of experiences and perspectives on EQ. As a professional therapist, John has worked extensively with religious leaders to develop their EQ and help them heal from the rigors of religious leadership. Roy has spent many years coaching and consulting with pastors and continues to work with them through the EQ-HR Center, an organization he cofounded. Nadyne's experience with EQ has come through her work as a university professor and as a leadership development consultant and coach. Additionally, both John and Roy have served as church pastors, and Nadyne's ministry is in hospital chaplaincy.

We believe that an opportunity exists for religious leaders to thrive in their work when they are given the tools of EQ. We offer this volume to help individual religious leaders face their current challenges and to promote their ongoing development. We also submit this work as a guide for Bible colleges, seminaries, and denominations as they adjust their curriculum and policies to meet the critical task of developing emotionally intelligent religious leaders. Our original hope was to create a resource that has not been available until now.

We recognize that the work of religious leaders is crucial to the spiritual development of individuals, and to the healing of society during a most challenging time in human history. We dedicate this book to you who work in religious leadership, and we thank you for your commitment to serve others. May your work be blessed!

John, Roy, and Nadyne

March 2018

I

INTRODUCTION

Today I visited someone who tried to commit suicide. Then I went to visit a baby whose mother had been doing drugs. The baby is blind, and her brain is not working properly. Her blood sugar is going up and down, up and down, up and down. I'm there with the grandparents, praying. That was my morning. Sometimes I just go sit downstairs and say, "God, come on, seriously?"

—Anonymous religious leader

For those of us who have served as religious leaders, this quote describes the terrible feeling of helplessness and frustration we have experienced many times in our career. We who have been called to serve as pastors, priests, chaplains, elders, administrators, teachers, or faith-based counselors (to name a few) have accepted a call to religious leadership, and we have decided to help others as they experience the inevitable vicissitudes and challenges of life. Many people have experienced loss or trauma, while others are in spiritual distress. Others are confused and discouraged as they earnestly search for a meaningful existence. The difficult work of religious leadership calls on us to be emotionally and spiritually grounded no matter what each situation brings.

The three of us (John, Roy, and Nadyne) bring different sets of experiences, perspectives, and understandings from our collective years of serving others in religious leadership. Along the way, each of us has learned about emotional intelligence (popularly known as EQ) and how it enhances the effectiveness of leadership, communication, and interrelationships in religious settings. And so we decided to create this book as a way of connecting with religious leaders who are ready to become emotionally and spiritually healthy and optimally effectual in their service to others.

Each of us approached the writing of this book from a Christian paradigm, and this perspective is undoubtedly reflected throughout the book. However, it is our intention for this work to be a guide for all religious leaders who would like to enhance their EQ. What we authors have in common with each other, and with you, is our call to be religious leaders and our resolute dedication to the precious human beings we have been called to serve. It is our sincere hope that this book will be a useful resource for EQ development and a source of help and encouragement during your challenging times of religious leadership.

WHAT IS EQ?

It's important for us to understand that religious leadership requires well-developed emotional intelligence, or EQ, skills. This is because so much of our work involves helping people with their emotional needs. EQ has been defined as the ability to monitor one's own and other people's emotions, to differentiate between different emotions and label them appropriately, and to use emotional information to guide thinking and behavior.[1] Otherwise stated, for us to productively perform our duties and survive the emotional rigors of religious leadership, we need to be able to identify, comprehend, and manage our emotions both internally and externally.[2] Put simply, EQ can help us to process our feelings and to address the emotions of others constructively.

EQ allows us to learn more about our emotional dimension and how to put this self-knowledge to beneficial use. As colorfully illustrated in the movie *Inside Out*, we are emotional beings with a wonderful blend of intense feelings that can be recognized and understood. Our emotions are closely tied to our life experiences, and our actions are profoundly affected by our feelings. In this book, we will address the benefits of EQ for us as religious leaders, both internally (within ourselves) and externally (working with others).

Emotional intelligence has progressively gained acceptance among scholars as a set of skills (also called competencies) that can be developed to improve ourselves.[3] EQ research has steadily advanced since it was first introduced in 1990 and especially after Daniel Goleman's 1995 watershed book, *Emotional Intelligence: Why It Can Matter More Than IQ*.[4] Goleman explained how the limbic system of the brain has tremendous power over our thinking patterns. He wrote that our feelings or emotions have major repercussions on our "thinking" brain, and EQ helps us to understand how our feelings greatly influence our decisions.

It's critical that we become emotionally and spiritually mature to assist others adequately. As one religious leader warned: "People aren't always emotionally healthy themselves when they are trying to help others. That's the problem when people go into the business of helping people." We have created this book to help you explore and expand your emotional intelligence, so you can serve others with the greatest positive result.

STRESSORS, RESILIENCE, AND EQ

As mentioned earlier, we wrote this book for all types of religious leaders who bear the emotional and spiritual burdens of others. Serving in religious leadership includes the enormous challenge of guiding people through their life choices, character development, and emotional difficulties. We committed our lives to this service so we could make a lasting impact on people. One religious leader said: "What I like most is being able to make a difference in people's lives. I like being able to accomplish something that will last beyond my lifetime and do something that really matters in people's hearts." It's true that working with people in this capacity is an amazing privilege. At times, religious leadership can be wondrous, even miraculous, as we watch people heal and grow. However, the process of helping people can take a great deal of emotional energy from us!

The need for religious leaders to have EQ is greater than for other professionals. Why? Because no other professional venue requires a person to manage as many emotional and spiritual burdens as are demanded by religious leadership. Our work challenges our internal fortitude, personal character, and individual resolve. It often requires us to exceed our limits and push ourselves into a state of compassion fatigue if we allow it.[5] As one religious leader elaborated: "If you are not filling up your own heart as you pour out your heart, then you are quickly empty, and you have nothing left to give. So you have to stay internally healthy in order to help other people."

Like Elijah (I Kings 19:4–14), we can easily succumb to feelings of being all alone in our leadership efforts, and find ourselves disheartened. Charles Spurgeon, known in the late-nineteenth century as the "Prince of Preachers," once described the great discouragement and intense depression he felt as a religious leader: "The ministry is a matter which wears the brain and strains the heart, and drains out the life of a [person] if [they] attend to it as [they] should."[6] One religious leader we interviewed summed up the emotional gravity of religious leadership this way: "The weight of the demands as a pastor are emotionally, and even physically taxing. I feel a constant anxiety: 'Wait, I've got to do this, I've got to plan for that, I've got to prepare this, I've got a sermon, I need to meet with that person.' All these things can weigh on you, and it can be crushing sometimes."

What is required of us, considering such professional stressors, is resilience, which allows us to adapt well when we face challenges. The trauma, tragedy, and hardship experienced by those we serve are serious threats to our emotional well-being because we are right there with them. We can also face our own stressors, such as family problems, financial issues, and serious health concerns. Fortunately, developing EQ skills helps us to improve our resilience because we can understand the emotional dynamics of others and process our own feelings in the face of adversity.

Religious leadership is incredibly complex and the expectations are often ambiguous. In other words, it can feel like our duties have no boundaries or limits. Being a "holy person" isn't exactly a helpful job description. Many people have high expectations of how we should serve them and what a "good" religious leader should look like. Ultimately, it falls on us to support them, guide them, counsel them, and accompany them through their most difficult situations. Emotional intelligence provides us with the tools to be an effective leader amid these extensive responsibilities.

EQ IS ESSENTIAL FOR RELIGIOUS AND SPIRITUAL LEADERSHIP

All professional leaders can benefit from EQ development, and we as religious leaders are certainly included in this group.[7] However, our roles as religious leaders are unique and carry more risk than other leaders because we operate within a sacred context. Because of this, we are responsible for the *spiritual* leadership of those we serve as a part of our larger role as religious leaders. In other words, we make a big impression on the spirituality of those we serve. When we as religious leaders establish effective EQ skills, we are more likely to have a positive influence on the people for whom we hold spiritual responsibility.[8]

We can better understand the essential role that religious leaders play in the spirituality of others by considering the relationship between coaches and their players. For example, coaches help players believe in themselves and their roles on the team, to develop their physical abilities, and to achieve their potential as athletes. As Ara Parseghian, former football coach of the Notre Dame Fighting Irish once said, "A good coach will make his players see what they can be, rather than what they are."

In the same way, religious leaders can apply traits of EQ to help others develop a deeper faith in God, grow as human beings, and lead a committed life of service. An example of this can be seen from Barnabas, who demonstrated EQ when Paul needed support at a pivotal time—and helped him to realize his spiritual potential (Acts 9:23–31). As religious leaders, we are similarly presented with key opportunities to foster growth in others. In these vital instances, we must use EQ if we hope to have a positive consequence on the spiritual maturity of those in our charge.

Our skill in EQ is what allows us to earn the trust of others and to create a connection that can empower their growth and ours. As Martin Buber wrote: "When two people relate to each other authentically and humanly, God is the electricity that surges between them."[9] Roy shared his extensive experience while coaching religious leaders:

> As I sometimes say to clergy, "You may not even like each other, but that should not prevent the two of you from developing a significant relationship. Following that kind of connectedness, whenever you encounter that person, the two of you smile at each other, knowing

that you have bonded in a special way. Without this kind of bonding, the two of you will look at ways to discredit each other, whether consciously or unconsciously."[10]

When we understand that we can positively affect our relationships by actively expanding our EQ, we take a huge step toward enhancing our religious leadership.

THE GAP BETWEEN THEOLOGICAL TRAINING AND RELIGIOUS LEADERSHIP

During our research, many interviewees explained to us that they were well trained in theology and religious instruction during their formal education. However, they also communicated that their theological and religious training alone wasn't enough to prepare them for the emotional rigor they faced as religious leaders (figure 1.1). As Roy wrote previously: "Pastoral ministry is all about relationships. You may be a brilliant theologian, excellent at biblical exegesis . . . but if you are not emotionally intelligent, your ministry . . . will be difficult."[11]

We believe that humans have been created by God as emotional beings; therefore, our decisions are processed through an emotional

Figure I.I.   Religious Leadership without Emotional Intelligence

filter. This emotional filter comprises a complicated combination of our life experiences, temperament, and core values. It has been stated that we are "more strongly driven by passions than directed by reason."[12] Because of this, if we hope to lead excellently, we are unable to process every scenario that we encounter on a purely informational or rational level. By ignoring our emotions, we will short-circuit our abilities and stunt our formation as religious leaders.

This isn't to say that we should ignore our intellect or training and allow our feelings to dictate all our leadership decisions. In fact, our heart can be misled, and we must also use our intellect to be balanced in our decision making (Jeremiah 17:9). We must "cultivate reason in emotion, as well as emotion in reason."[13] Our theological training (mind) and emotional center (heart) must both be involved if we hope to lead others toward growth and to maintain our own emotional and spiritual health.

As Roy explained in a previous work, religious leaders must endeavor to "blend rationality and emotionality in ways that are truly transformative."[14] In so doing, we can create a powerful nexus of our head and heart in our leadership decisions. This optimal combination can be discovered by developing our emotional intelligence because EQ acts as an invaluable guide for our theological training. It also helps us tremendously when religious leadership feels burdensome (figure 1.2).

Most of the religious leaders we interviewed expressed that the Bible colleges and seminaries they attended did not include EQ training as a part of their formal education.[15] As a result, they were forced to advance their EQ skills through nontraditional training opportunities such as outside coaching, professional therapy, and self-study. In this book, we provide religious leaders with a valuable resource to develop their EQ traits. We hope that this will serve as a survival guide for religious leaders, so that each of you will flourish as you faithfully fulfill your calling. The development of EQ is a lifelong process through which we mature emotionally and spiritually and during which we set aside our "childish ways" (I Corinthians 13:11, NRSV).

Figure I.2.   Religious Leadership with Emotional Intelligence

EXPLANATION OF OUR RESEARCH AND STRUCTURE

We began our preparation for this book by studying the eighteen competencies originally identified by Daniel Goleman and his colleagues (table 1.1).[16] Based on their research and professional experience working with and interviewing religious leaders, we narrowed down the eighteen competencies to six traits we believe are most essential for religious leadership: (1) Emotional Self-Awareness, (2) Emotional Self-Control, (3) Empathy, (4) Organizational Awareness, (5) Influence, and (6) Conflict Management. Our emphasis on these six traits is not in any way meant to indicate that the remaining twelve are unimportant to those serving in religious leadership. We chose to narrow down the EQ development process so we can focus on those traits we believe are most urgent for religious leaders in their work. These pivotal traits are listed in bold type in table 1. In later chapters, we delve more deeply into these six traits.

Since our research determined that the trait of Emotional Self-Awareness is foundational to the EQ of religious leaders, we have dedicated chapters 2 and 3 to the discussion of this crucial topic. We have also included a culminating chapter (chapter 9), "Spirituality of the Emotionally Intelligent Religious Leader." This chapter ties together all six of the EQ traits covered in this book and explains how religious leaders can advance their spirituality to enhance their religious leadership. However, we invite you to skim this chapter in advance if you would like a "sneak preview" of how the traits come together to create a positive relationship between your development in EQ and your spirituality.

Table 1.1.   The Four Domains of Emotional Intelligence

Domain	Competencies
Self-Awareness	**Emotional Self-Awareness**
	Accurate Self-Assessment
	Self-Confidence
Self-Management	**Emotional Self-Control**
	Transparency
	Adaptability
	Achievement
	Initiative
	Optimism
Social Awareness	**Empathy**
	Organizational Awareness
	Service
Relationship Management	Inspirational Leadership
	Influence
	Developing Others
	Change Catalyst
	Conflict Management
	Teamwork and Collaboration

MOVING FORWARD

We have organized this book so that readers can (1) understand how the various EQ traits affect their interpersonal relationships and the effectiveness of their religious leadership; (2) create a plan for improving their EQ skills in the areas of Emotional Self-Awareness, Emotional Self-Control, Empathy, Organizational Awareness, Influence, and Conflict Management; (3) focus on themselves to expand their potential as spiritual leaders of individuals and faith communities; and (4) experience profound satisfaction in their work.

As a reader, you will find the progression of these topics flows naturally through the six areas of EQ as they are presented. Just remember this: the development of EQ does not occur in a linear or sequential manner. The process of emotional and spiritual growth is often circuitous and reflexive, especially as our understanding of EQ strengthens and deepens. As you embark on this remarkable adventure of EQ exploration, we encourage you to be mindful of how your internal perceptions and external relationships grow and mature and what effect this growth has on your religious and spiritual leadership.

2

EMOTIONAL SELF-AWARENESS AS A FOUNDATION

The only people who grow in truth are those who are humble and honest.

—Fr. Richard Rohr[1]

Each of us (John, Roy, and Nadyne) has admitted to each other that we've had moments in our lives that were not only imprudent but were contrary to our values—and we wondered *why*. At the time of our actions, we lacked the self-knowledge to consider how our unconscious needs and ego had caused us to behave in ways that were destructive, hurtful, or counterproductive. Each of us has shared the sentiment of the anonymous religious leader, who said: "If only I had known myself better." From these experiences, we've learned what Daniel Goleman and others have asserted: emotional self-awareness is the foundation of EQ, which, in turn, is essential to effective religious leadership.[2]

WHAT IS EMOTIONAL SELF-AWARENESS?

The trait of Emotional Self-Awareness is an enduring concept. For example, Jesus encouraged emotional self-awareness in his disciples, as shown in Matthew 7:3–5 (NIV):

> Why do you look at the speck of sawdust in your brother's eye and pay no attention to the plank in your own eye? How can you say to

your brother, "Let me take the speck out of your eye," when all the time there is a plank in your own eye? You hypocrite, first take the plank out of your own eye, and then you will see clearly to remove the speck from your brother's eye.

We are further encouraged to seek emotional self-awareness in Proverbs 20:5 (NIV): "The purposes of a person's heart are deep waters, but one who has insight draws them out." Other examples of emotional self-awareness can be found among the ancient literature, including "know thyself" from the Oracle at Delphi,[3] self-assessment and military strategy from Sun Tzu,[4] and wrestling with our spiritual self from the African-Igbo parable.[5]

The trait of Emotional Self-Awareness is the cornerstone of emotional intelligence. It helps us to understand ourselves in ways that aren't known to those who lack this trait. With emotional self-awareness, we learn what triggers us emotionally when working with other people, why these visceral impulses can be so intense, and how to address these emotional responses in a healthy way. Without it, our judgment can become clouded by emotional baggage and our leadership can be impaired. One religious leader explained:

> When I was younger, there were those feelings that were much more intense, and I would have probably acted on them. I now know how I am wired, so that's helpful, I think. But I know that comes with time and experience and taking some time to learn who you are, and to understand yourself.

As we develop emotional self-awareness, we understand why certain feelings occur under various circumstances. It helps us to describe the underlying reasons for our feelings, and how our perception of reality activates our emotions and influences our behaviors. Although we aren't always able to discover the reasons we feel the way we do, we can learn at a minimum to manage our emotions and how they affect our leadership decisions. The trait of Emotional Self-Awareness is defined as: "reading one's own emotions and recognizing their impact; using [one's] 'gut sense' to guide decisions."[6]

In the following sections, we discuss some of the reasons the EQ trait of Emotional Self-Awareness is uniquely significant for religious leaders. Please note: this chapter focuses on psychological and philosophical concepts that may be emotionally challenging. We encourage you to persevere with this chapter because these foundational concepts are referenced throughout this book and are essential to your overall work of developing EQ. If needed, pace yourself as you digest the personal significance of what you are reading and how it applies to your role as a religious leader.

CONCEPT OF THE CALLING

Religious leaders have a unique understanding of what it feels like to have a "calling from God." A calling is a phenomenon experienced by those who feel an intense, persistent, divinely inspired compulsion to live in service to others as their long-term profession. It is defined as "the unmistakable conviction an individual possesses that God wants him [or her] to do a specific task."[7] Receiving a calling is a sacred concept: "Then I heard the voice of the Lord saying, 'Whom shall I send, and who will go for us?' And I said, 'Here am I; send me!'" (Isaiah 6:8, NRSV). We can also identify with the disciples and the Great Commission: "Go therefore and make disciples of all nations, baptizing them in the name of the Father and of the Son and of the Holy Spirit, and teaching them to obey everything that I have commanded you" (Matthew 28:19, NRSV).

The call can look different for each religious leader. It can be something akin to God speaking to Saul on the road to Damascus, speaking in a "still, small voice" to Elijah, or grabbing our attention with measures that seem as drastic as Jonah and his great fish. Sometimes our call feels very dramatic, such as in the classic movie *Sergeant York*, whose main character was struck by lightning as part of his conversion experience. Regardless of how we each experienced our initial calling, it can feel like a tremendous amount of work and sacrifice to meet God's expectation of us.

Our call can be a wonderful part of our lives; however, we can also be hurt by a misguided expectation of martyrdom that we place on ourselves. For many of us, this teaching began in our formal education, where we were taught the stories of first-century believers who gave their lives for the Christian cause. Some of us were also inspired by Jim Elliot, who was slain by the native Huaorani tribe in Ecuador where he served as a missionary. Elliot's famous quote has been taught to many young religious students: "He is no fool who gives what he cannot keep to gain that which he cannot lose."[8]

Fortunately, most of us don't carry an expectation of literal martyrdom; however, many of us do expect to live a life of extreme sacrifice.[9] This paradigm can become problematic, even dangerous, as we face the emotional challenges inherent with helping others. Because people are never fully grown or healed, we can feel as though our work is never finished. It feels like the quote from the movie *The Incredibles*:

> No matter how many times you save the world, it always manages to get back in jeopardy again. Sometimes I just want it to stay saved! You know, for a little bit? I feel like the maid; I just cleaned up this mess! Can we keep it clean for . . . for ten minutes?![10]

Without emotional self-awareness, we will never find the proper balance between what God expects of us and the unrealistic expectations we place on ourselves. We need emotional self-awareness to help us identify when our desire to serve has become tainted by deep-seated issues such as existential debt, ego battles, and perfectionism.

EXISTENTIAL DEBT

Most of us dedicate our lives to helping people because we feel a healthy responsibility to serve others. However, our reasons to serve can also include an unconscious attempt to "right the wrongs" of our past. This obligation can be due to childhood trauma and corresponding feelings of guilt, which motivate us to serve others in an attempt to repay this perceived debt.[11] For example, a child who lost a parent might enter a life of religious leadership due to a deep-seated need to rescue others since he or she was unable to save the parent.

In my case (John), I lost my mother to suicide when I was a small boy. It wasn't until I had served in religious leadership for many years that I realized I was motivated to rescue others as a surrogate for my mom—whom I was unable to save. This realization didn't negate the importance of the religious leadership I performed in my adult life, nor did it diminish the value I added to others' lives. It did, however, help me to decrease the instances I overcommitted myself. Instead of grieving over every congregant who departed from my ministry, I learned that it isn't my job to save everyone. I realized that my role is to serve faithfully and communicate God's message only to those people who are within my sphere of influence.

For me (Nadyne), it began when, as a young child, I enjoyed the praise I received when I acted kindly or put the needs of others before my own. Because I was punished severely for any "selfish" actions, I learned how to behave "correctly." And so anytime I found myself straying from the path of taking care of others first, I felt guilty and anxious and disapproving of myself, thus laying the foundation for my existential debt. Before long I was on the path of service. Adding to the complexity of my need to succeed and to be seen positively in the eyes of others was my experience of living in the Southwest as a Mexican American in the 1950s and 1960s. I was often confused and saddened by the rejections I experienced from others, so I just tried harder to be seen as a kind person. As an adult, it became apparent that I was driven to serve others who had experienced rejection and marginalization in any form. Eventually, I learned how important it is also to take care of my physical, emotional, and spiritual needs so that I can live a balanced and healthy life and serve others from a place of compassion, not personal need.

I (Roy) entered seminary not knowing why. In retrospect, my decision was for all the wrong reasons, yet I never regretted my choice. My father was a "fire and brimstone" Lutheran preacher, and I thought that if I didn't go to seminary, I would spend eternity in hell. I was doing it to save my soul. I spent most of my growing-up years figuring out what other people needed, and I tried to give that to them. I was a natural do-gooder, trying to please everyone. However, when I became an adolescent, I experienced great conflict between my desire to serve God and a growing sexuality that overwhelmed me at times. I entered seminary in hopes that my sex drive would diminish. My image of seminary was that of entering some kind of holy order that would help me manage this unholy state. Boy, was I surprised when my academic training was steeped in Bible and theology instead of the positive spiritual experience that I expected. However, my first experience as a Lutheran parish pastor and chaplain for students began a whole new chapter of my life. It was then that I truly understood my calling and I haven't turned back since.

Developing our emotional self-awareness can help us understand our reasons for entering religious leadership. It can also help us keep the demands of religious leadership in proper perspective, and protect us from unhealthy habits, such as overcommitment, self-neglect, and people pleasing. In short, it keeps us from attempting to accomplish more than we should and from working ourselves to death.

EGO AND HUBRIS

Many of the religious leaders we interviewed explained that they often need to check their ego, so that it doesn't unduly sway their attitude and decisions. It's worth noting that the ego isn't something we can eliminate; it is a permanent part of us. In this book, we make the distinction between "ego" and "ego strength." We recognize that each of us must develop sufficient ego strength (which is a strong and necessary sense of self) to bear the emotional and spiritual burdens inherent in religious leadership.[12] In contrast, the "ego" is defined as "that part of the self that wants to be significant, central, and important by itself, apart from anybody else. The ego wants to be both separate and superior, and it is defensive and self-protective by its very nature."[13]

Our ego is like a full-time litigator that persistently mounts a vigorous defense on our behalf. It is quick to plead our case over any perceived slight, perception of failure, or challenge to our moral high ground. Simply stated, our ego is insecure and hypervigilant at its very core, and unable to abide any perception of fault.[14] Father Richard Rohr, a Franciscan priest and theologian, explained that our ego's primary aim is to eliminate all negative feedback, so that we can feel blameless and superior to others.[15]

Because of our ego's questionable influence, our attitude and corresponding behavior can be adversely affected in subtle, but significant ways. Our ego can also be described as an insatiably hungry teenager with the proverbial bottomless stomach. As such, it continuously tries to sate our psychological hunger by proving that we are unassailably worthwhile. Some examples of our ego-driven attitudes and behaviors include:

- We need to prove we are "right" most of the time.

- We find ourselves in arguments regarding the existence of God with nonbelievers.
- We find ourselves being highly critical of other Christians and other religions because they don't adhere to our beliefs or our religious code.
- We worry about one of our staff members or coworkers supplanting us in our position.
- We fret about other people taking credit for our ideas.
- We are often concerned about looking foolish or making an embarrassing mistake.
- We find ourselves in continual disputes with church members regarding scriptural interpretations or teachings.
- We have difficulty giving credit to other people for their ideas.
- We struggle with admitting we are wrong and/or with apologizing for it.
- We are inflexible with our agenda or plans at work, or unable to incorporate the input of others.
- We are unhappy unless we feel we are winning or beating someone else.
- We only feel successful when our ministry grows numerically.
- We hold grudges against those we feel have wronged us.
- We worry excessively about what others think of us.

Our ego also maintains a close relationship with hubris or excessive pride. Hubris occurs for us when our ego becomes inflated by our accomplishments. Once hubris infects our attitude, it can be difficult to remember the good reasons we answered our call. As one religious leader confessed, "I was guilty. Pride and self-importance were all wrapped up and twisted in with passion, commitment, and a desire to serve." Developing emotional self-awareness grants us the opportunity to reflect on how these obsessions of ego can pollute our attitude toward religious leadership. Namely, we begin to comprehend that not all our behavior may be motivated for altruistic reasons.

We can be tempted to build our empire, carve out a legacy, or strive to accomplish "great things." Unfortunately, this attitude of self-promotion can dilute our call and damage our leadership. Left unchecked, our ego will drive us to become our own worst enemy. As Rocky Balboa told his protégé while training in front of the mirror: "You see this guy staring back at you? That's your toughest opponent. I believe that's true in the ring, and I think that's true in life."[16] And so it's essential for us to remain aware of how our ego can lead us into temptation and taint the purity of our call. King Solomon provided insight into this trap: "Pride goes before destruction, and a haughty spirit before a fall" (Proverbs 16:18, ESV). One religious leader explained their experience:

> My heart still aches for a place to be needed, to contribute, to play a part in the great things going on, to meet the needs of others. And this, in itself, isn't bad. But if you add the small bit of honesty I'm allowing myself, I'd also have to admit that my heart aches for power, prestige and status.

HUMILITY

The antidote for an inflamed ego and excessive pride is humility, as explained in Proverbs 11:2 (NLT): "Pride leads to disgrace, but with humility comes wisdom." Indeed, Jesus taught us the importance of humility over self-aggrandizement when he taught that "the first will be last, and the last will be first" (Matthew 20:16, NIV). With humility, we know who we are and realize we are doing our best. Then we can find peace and balance between our victories and defeats, gains and losses, triumphs and failures. True humility relieves the tension between striving to become exemplary religious leaders and knowing our limitations. In short, we are unable to increase our emotional self-awareness without a humble attitude. It's simply too painful to look closely at ourselves without it.

Living within the endeavors of our call creates an interesting paradox. The harder we try to become righteous people, the more tempted we are to evaluate ourselves as better than others. Unfortunately, the more we try to be "good" Christians, the further we stray from spiritual maturity. However, once we learn to accept ourselves as flawed human beings, living among similarly faulty people, our sense of self can gain equilibrium. It's at that point we can find emotional and spiritual rest because our ego can relax. As Thomas Merton wrote, "pride makes us artificial, and humility makes us real."[17] Buddhist philosophy reinforces the importance of this balance: "When things are going well, be mindful of adversity . . . when respected, be mindful of humility."[18]

In the pursuit of humility, we must be cautious not to allow our ego to become crushed, lest we experience humiliation or toxic shame.[19] With humility we can maintain our dignity; however, with humiliation, we can perceive ourselves to be worthless and useless. We can find the proper balance between the two when we consider that we are sanctified and called by God in service of others. We can then learn to be kind to ourselves and others, despite and because of our humanness: "Therefore, as God's chosen people, holy and dearly loved, clothe yourselves with compassion, kindness, humility, gentleness, and patience" (Colossians 3:12, NIV). Humility, then, comes from an honest and gentle reckoning and acceptance of our foibles and imperfections.

As religious leaders, we are under tremendous pressure to be superhuman. However, we only need to be at peace with our status as God's children (Galatians 3:26), who clothes us with grace (Titus 3:5–7). The acceptance of our good standing with God effectively releases our ego from its relentless pursuit of absolution. Then we can understand what John Eldridge meant when he encouraged us to be authentic and transparent: "Let people feel the full weight of who you are, and let [others] deal with it."[20] Emotional self-awareness permits us to learn more fully about ourselves and safely accept what we discover, whether we consider it to be attractive or unattractive. As we embrace authenticity and transparency, humility can emerge in our character as a natural phenomenon that releases us from the curse of hubris and our inflated ego.

PERFECTIONISM

It is so easy to expect too much of ourselves as religious leaders. In part, we expect ourselves to be perfect because we are supposed to set an excellent example for others. Additionally, we push ourselves to be perfect because we feel that God expects this from us. However, only God is perfect, and pursuing the illusion of perfection is emotionally and spiritually destructive (Mark 10:18; Romans 3:23).

Perfectionism is based on dualistic thinking, that we are either good OR bad people. Unfortunately, our self-perception often gets stuck on the gloomy side of this scale. In some instances, this can lead either to a pattern of overachievement, or to a state of paralysis in which we can't

make decisions at all. Here are a few examples of perfectionism that
religious leaders experience:

- We beat ourselves up when we make a mistake.
- We never feel as if we have accomplished enough to rest.
- We blame ourselves every time a congregant is unhappy.
- We believe that every problem can be fixed if a little more effort
  is applied.
- We believe every job should be done exactly right, or not at-
  tempted at all.
- We worry whether our decisions have kept us in God's favor, or if
  we have fallen out of God's will.

Jonathan Kellerman insightfully captured how it feels for those afflicted with perfectionism: "You set extremely high standards for yourself, and when you succeed, you ignore the success and immediately
raise your standards. But when you fail, you won't let go of it. You keep
punishing yourself, telling yourself you're worthless."[21]

Once perfectionism infects our heart and mind, it influences us to
demand excellence and faultlessness from ourselves and everyone
around us. However, the focus of our work is with human beings, and
humanity is imperfect. Therefore, our work can never be perfect. Because of this, we must have compassion for others and ourselves, or
religious leadership will continually feel like a no-win situation.

OUR FALSE SELF

When we create an internal system of perfectionism to hide our flaws,
we simultaneously create an external "false self." Unfortunately, this
disguise tends to be common among religious leaders. The high expectations of others, along with our internal drive to be blameless, combine
to create enormous pressure on us. As mentioned above, the relief
valves for this pressure are humility, transparency, and authenticity.[22]

Unfortunately, we have a natural tendency to conceal our shortcomings, just as Adam did in the Garden of Eden (Genesis 3:6–8). As a
result, we tend to display a false self to protect ourselves from judg-

ment. The essence of the false self was lyrically captured in the novel *Freedom of the Mask*:

> His face was a mask, showing no emotion. It was all locked within, and perhaps that was a freedom of the mask . . . the ability to show the world a false face, while holding all the torment deep inside, to show the world in essence a false person, a construct of circumstance.[23]

Regrettably, our false self is an artificial construct, and it lacks the full weight and power contained within our authentic self. Performing our demanding duties while simultaneously maintaining a false face takes an enormous amount of energy. For example, it takes a toll on us to maintain the pretense of perfection in an emotionally charged work environment. Also, hiding our emotions prevents us from gaining healthy relationships with others because it prevents them from truly knowing us.

When we hide behind a façade, we become an example of inauthenticity. After attempting to act as a perfect person for a time, we eventually come to proclaim: "Spare me perfection. Give me instead the wholeness that comes from embracing the full reality of who I am."[24] Once we embrace our authentic selves, we no longer feel the burden of "faking it," or wonder if others would like us if they really knew us. As Donald Miller wrote: "It feels better to have people love the real me than the me I invented."[25]

THE SHADOW

Carl Jung's concept of the shadow is also helpful as we learn to accept ourselves as complicated people, complete with good and bad qualities.[26] Those of us who are Christians believe that we are spiritually transformed by Christ into something new (2 Corinthians 5:17). However, our spiritual metamorphosis doesn't countermand the imperfection of our humanity (Romans 7:15–19; 12:2). It can be confusing for us to understand why we still possess a "dark side," despite our spiritual and emotional growth. The concept of the shadow was Jung's way of describing those elements that we wish to deny and keep hidden, even from ourselves.

We must learn to accept ourselves as imperfect or our shadow will find unhealthy forms of expression. When this happens, our shadow can erupt from its place of dormancy with severely destructive behavior and with terrible human consequences, just like the devastation wreaked upon the ancient Roman city of Pompeii by the once-dormant volcano Mount Vesuvius. The novelist Troy Denning aptly referred to this dangerous phenomenon as a shadow crisis.[27] Such emotional eruptions are caused by the visceral impulses we keep locked away, which are eventually brought to light by emotional "triggers." Fortunately, the pursuit of emotional self-awareness can help us identify and address these shadow elements before they sabotage our relationships and impair our leadership.

Once we learn to accept that our "unacceptable" qualities don't make us terrible individuals, we can begin to accept the full spectrum of our humanity. Jung fittingly described this process as the integration of the personality.[28] This process of integration ultimately makes us stronger and healthier people, freeing us from a restrictive black-and-white philosophy that requires us to be characterized as either good or bad people. As the novelist Lisa Fantino poetically expressed: "Each of us lives in the grey zone, in the shadows between precise and unknowing."[29]

With EQ, we can learn to reveal our authentic selves and overcome our fear of being judged. The removal of our mask also allows us to build increased levels of trust and influence. Remember, we must first learn to be authentic with ourselves before we can be authentic with others. Then we can set an emotionally honest example for people to follow. As one religious leader said, "honesty and transparency are the best resources in my bag of tricks."[30]

By allowing ourselves to be "perfectly imperfect," we open our hearts to a gentle self-perspective that includes our shadow. It requires courage to face the less attractive facets of our self that violate our perception of "good," whether the measuring stick comes from religious or societal norms. "One of the great surprises on the human journey is that we come to full consciousness precisely by shadowboxing, facing our own contradictions, and making friends with our own mistakes and failings."[31]

It's essential that we learn to accept ourselves as individuals whose process of emotional and spiritual growth will always remain unfinished. With this perspective, we can humbly learn the lessons that God intends for us and experience the joy of knowing that God is continually working in our lives. Once we embrace this idea, our religious leadership can grow in ways we can scarcely imagine, as we move steadily toward emotional and spiritual maturity.

CONCLUSION

Without emotional self-awareness, we lack the resources needed to address our own emotional confusion, much less handle the complex emotional and spiritual problems faced by others. By increasing our emotional self-awareness, we can learn our strengths and weaknesses, purify our motivation for serving others, and find peace with the entirety of our personality and humanness. The pursuit of emotional self-awareness requires humility and courage, yet it is a most worthwhile endeavor that can strengthen us and increase our effectiveness in service to others.

3

DEVELOPING EMOTIONAL SELF-AWARENESS

I wish I knew myself better.

—Anonymous pastor

While the quote above came from an interview we conducted, all three of us have uttered or shouted these same words more than once in our lives. The bit we shared about ourselves in chapter 2 should give you an indication of our humanness—and our awareness of our vulnerabilities. We have each been on a journey that's been both challenging and satisfying, although each step has led to another discovery that brought with it another challenge. That is the nature of emotional and spiritual development, as you have undoubtedly realized.

In chapter 2 we established the importance of the foundational EQ trait of Emotional Self-Awareness for religious leaders. We also highlighted the challenges and benefits inherent in the process of developing self-awareness. And yes, it can be an endeavor that is both daunting and complex. Fortunately, we have discovered that multiple resources are available to help us in the quest to increase emotional self-awareness. In this chapter, we explore several of these options that facilitate growth in this pivotal EQ trait. Resources we recommend include temperament and personality-type assessments, strategies for gaining internal perspective, and techniques for soliciting feedback and guidance from others. We have personally utilized everything we share here in our own lives.

TEMPERAMENT THEORY AND PERSONALITY TYPE

One of the primary ways we can develop our emotional self-awareness is by studying the concept of temperament theory. The main premise of temperament theory is that each person is hard-wired at birth with specific personality characteristics. Through greater understanding of temperament theory, we learn a great deal about ourselves, including an increased knowledge of our strengths and weaknesses.

Temperament theory originated from the ancient teachings of Hippocrates, who offered a four-part theory of temperament assessment and categorization. This theory has since been refined and widely disseminated by various modern psychologists and authors. Many testing instruments are available that religious leaders can utilize to assess their temperament, including the Myers-Briggs Type Indicator, Keirsey Temperament Sorter, Profile of Ministry, DISC Personality Profile, and StrengthsFinder.

Among these, one of the most commonly known personality-assessment tools is the Myers-Briggs Type Indicator (MBTI). The MBTI categorizes each person's personality according to four key indicators.

1. Extraversion (E) vs. Introversion (I)
2. Sensing (S) vs. Intuition (N)
3. Thinking (T) vs. Feeling (F)
4. Judging (J) vs. Perceiving (P)

More information about the temperament indicators can be found at http://www.myersbriggs.org/my-mbti-personality-type/mbti-basics.

Using the MBTI or other temperament-assessment tools available, we learn more about ourselves and how we gather information, how we make decisions, and how we operate in the world. In short, we gain self-awareness of how we are mentally and emotionally designed. We begin to understand why we thrive in certain elements of the ministry and struggle with other aspects. Without this self-awareness, we lack understanding of why some duties of the ministry are more challenging for us. Temperament analysis also teaches us about what motivates our temperament type. Not only can we learn what motivates our specific temperament, but we can also gain an understanding of what motivates other people connected to our ministerial work. Understanding the temperament types of others, and how different temperaments might react to one another, can help us greatly in our interactions with the people we serve, teammates, board members, and denominational leaders.

A more complex tool for self-knowledge is the Enneagram. It is based upon nine interconnected personality types and has been synthesized from many spiritual and religious traditions, dating back to ancient Middle Eastern and Asian civilizations. The heart of the Enneagram is based on a universal perspective that human beings are spiritual presences incarnated in the natural world while embodying the same life and spirit as our creator; the light of God shines in every individual.[1] The Enneagram acknowledges that humans are born with certain temperaments—specific needs that are either met or thwarted through early experiences. From these experiences, our human personality is formed. However, the Enneagram conveys that we are more than the limitations of our personality. It's within our *essence* that we find our true nature. Our personality is merely one aspect of who we are. Using one of the tools developed by modern experts on the Enneagram, we can discover our "type" and other factors that affect how we think, feel, and behave. The Enneagram Institute describes the nine personality types on their website, https://www.enneagraminstitute.com/type-descriptions. Additionally, Richard Rohr details the weaknesses of each Enneagram type in his video workshop, *The Enneagram: The Discernment of Spirits.*[2]

Learning about ourselves by studying the Enneagram can expose our "shadow," as discussed in chapter 2. This can be an uncomfortable or embarrassing epiphany as we first experience this discovery process. We usually wrestle with the dark, shadowy elements of our "type" over the course of our lives; however, learning the specifics of our type increases our emotional self-awareness, and provides us with the choice to nurture and emphasize the positive elements of our personality in our daily lives. Any discomfort we experience in this or any other process of self-discovery is an essential component needed for our goal of increased emotional self-awareness. The Enneagram can further serve as a guide for psychological and spiritual growth *if we pursue it beyond learning the basic components of our type.*

It's vital to know that the use of these tools for learning about our temperament or personality type should not be limited to a short-term, cursory experience. Just taking an inventory on our own, and reading about our type, will only begin our self-discovery. This experience is much more enlightening, and more likely to change our behaviors, when we are guided over time by a professional who is trained and certified in the use of such tools.

Eventually, we can understand temperament theory well enough to teach others in our organization so that our interactions can become healthier and more effective. However, both the MBTI and the Enneagram are based on complex theories and should be administered to others only after special training with experts. Workshops and online classes are available for certification in these tools through a variety of training groups, including the MBTI Training Institute http://www.mbtitraininginstitute.myersbriggs.org and the Enneagram Institute http://www.enneagraminstitute.com.

GAINING INTERNAL PERSPECTIVE

Meditation

A principal method to learn about ourselves comes from the exercise of reflective meditation, an ancient practice that predates Christianity in both Jewish and Buddhist traditions. Meditation involves quieting our mind for a period, which allows us to be mindful of our body sensations, our thoughts and feelings, and our spiritual condition. This practice can be very difficult for us to justify as a habitual exercise due to the intensity of our schedules, and the continuous interruptions that encroach upon our attention span. It's this very lack of "quiet time" that prevents us from recognizing internal warning signs and emotional signposts that can prevent us from missteps in our personal and professional lives. By learning to look within to discover more about ourselves, we exchange our "mask" for a mirror, and carefully make an honest inventory of our heart's condition. In so doing, we understand the proclamation of the anonymous author: "When you are looking in the mirror, you are looking at the problem. But, remember, you are also looking at the solution."

Perhaps the paramount benefit of meditation is that it provides the opportunity for God to communicate to us, and to commune with us.

When we become too busy doing God's work to spend quality time with God, we become like Martha, who was busy preparing the event in Jesus's honor, rather than Mary, who spent time at Jesus's feet "listening to what he said" (Luke 10:38–42, NIV). One of the integral parts of meditation can include first reading Scripture or devotional material, which prepares our heart and mind for spiritual messages and emotional clarity.

Another element of meditation involves finding a peaceful place that limits outside stimulation, such as secluding ourselves in a quiet space in our house, at work (such as in the sanctuary at church), or by attending a spiritual retreat. Regarding the importance of meditation, the psalmist said: "May my meditation be pleasing to him, for I rejoice in the Lord" (Psalms 104:34, ESV). Through meditation, we can contemplate our emotional and spiritual discoveries, and allow these revelations to become the material needed for us to grow and increase our emotional and spiritual maturity.

Those who are unfamiliar with meditation would be well advised to seek instruction on how to proceed successfully. A variety of books, recordings, webinars, blogs, and classes are available on the topic of meditation that can be found using a simple Internet search.

Contemplative Prayer

Along with meditation, we can rediscover the lost art of *apophatic* prayer, which is sometimes referred to as contemplative prayer. This is currently practiced in monasteries, convents, and contemplative prayer centers throughout the world. Apophatic prayer differs from the common practice of kataphatic prayer (figure 3.1). With kataphatic prayer, we communicate with God through private and group prayers, liturgies, and hymns. Scripture encourages us to speak directly to God in supplication, praise, thanksgiving, confession, intercession, and so on, and these types of prayers should not be discouraged from our spiritual practice (Philippians 4:6–7; I John 1:9). However, the risk of practicing solely kataphatic prayer is that it provides little opportunity to listen to God. With apophatic prayer, we reverse the direction and energy of our prayers and attempt to put ourselves in a receptive mode of spiritual communication. As Manney wrote: "Apophatic prayer has no content. It means emptying the mind of words and ideas and simply resting in the presence of God."[3] The basic idea of apophatic prayer is to allow God to guide us in a "still, small voice" (I Kings 19:11–13).

The best way to understand the contrast between kataphatic and apophatic prayer is to picture them at opposite ends of a polarity. Spending time in both kataphatic and apophatic prayer is essential to a healthy prayer life, and we can move back and forth between each pole to meet our full range of needs. Apophatic prayer is the best choice for developing our emotional self-awareness because it gives us the opportunity to listen to and allow God to guide our emotional reactions and life decisions. Apophatic prayer is also a powerful way for us to build our relationship with God.

When preparing ourselves to listen to God in contemplative prayer, we must first be able to listen to our own mind, heart, body, and spirit. Cynthia Bourgeault describes this type of prayer as "consenting to the presence and action of God."[4] This practice requires us to become increasingly mindful and observant of the thoughts, feelings, and bodily sensations that are active at any given moment. Predictably, our ego often produces resistance when we begin this process, and our attention

Connection with God	
• We speak to God • Sending words and images to God • Liturgy • Hymnody • Private and group prayer • Communicate our feelings to God • Praise and thanksgiving to God	• God speaks to us • Meditation • Contemplative prayer • God is in the still, small voice • Open to revelation about ourselves • Open to learning about God • Our mind is unencumbered by self
▲ method/benefits **Kataphatic Prayer** ▼ risks	▲ method/benefits **Apophatic Prayer** ▼ risks
• Little emphasis on listening to God • We assume God doesn't want to speak to us • We are taught to send requests to God • We are not taught how to heed God's guidance	• Our prayer life can become too passive, open, and unfocused • We do not bring our requests or concerns to God • We forget what Jesus taught us: "Ask and you shall receive; knock and it will be opened to you"
Alienation from God	

Figure 3.1.   Apophatic versus Kataphatic Spirituality

can be easily diverted as we are reminded of our daily responsibilities, relational challenges, and personal agendas. For example, a memory of an offense from a coworker might come to mind and disrupt our meditative process. These disturbances similarly prevent us from listening to God and from receiving his daily communication to us. However, once we learn to discipline ourselves to listen in silence, our emotional self-awareness can increase considerably. This gives us key sources of internal reflection and insight.

Integrating into our prayer life the practice of listening to God has been referred to as "two-way prayer" as described in Step 11 of the Twelve Steps of Alcoholics Anonymous (AA).[5] With two-way prayer, we do not spend all our prayers speaking to God. Rather, we give God a turn to speak. As with any conversation between two people, the emotional connection is stronger when both sides have been heard. By listening to God, who guides us as a loving parent, we grow emotionally and spiritually in ways we would not gain otherwise (Romans 8:14).

The Big Book from AA provides a simple test to determine if our practice of meditation and contemplative prayer is allowing God to communicate with us, or if we are imposing the agenda of our ego.[6] After praying about what's on our mind, we can write down our thoughts. "When we finish our 'quiet time,' we check what we have on paper. If what we have written is *honest, pure, unselfish*, and *loving*, we can be assured that these thoughts are God directed. Conversely, if what we have written is *dishonest, resentful, selfish*, or *fearful*, we can be equally assured that these thoughts are self-centered" (AA, Step 11).

For many of us, the skills of meditation and contemplative prayer have been neglected in our formal education. This is possibly because we are expected to lead prayer in public settings as part of our ministerial duties. However, it's never too late for us to develop our facility in contemplative prayer. Ideally, we can learn to integrate both listening and speaking to God in a reflexive daily practice.

Journaling

Another practical method for us to engage in self-reflection is through journaling. This process involves writing down how we feel about the impactful events and occurrences in our life. The mechanical process of writing in a journal allows our mind and heart to process our thoughts and feelings uniquely and healthily.[7] For some, preserving the content of their journal entries may provide a profound resource for future reflection as a type of emotional history book. For those who greatly value their privacy, keeping such a personal record available for possible discovery creates an unacceptable risk. If this is a concern, privacy can be maintained by destroying each journal entry—or by writing each entry in code, such as using only the first letter of each word to obscure the meaning of the journal text from unwanted readers.

To begin journaling for the first time, it may help to utilize a script. An effective way to begin journal writing is with this simple template: I feel _____ about _____ because _____. This basic process allows us to identify what we are feeling, and why we feel that way. For some, this will be a new activity, and it will take practice to recognize each emotion. It may help to utilize the Feeling Wheel[8] or a similar chart that lists different emotions for a frame of reference. The format of the journal may be written in structured paragraphs, free form, or even as poetry. Another method that can stimulate journal writing includes beginning with a quote, a written devotional, or a picture as a source of inspiration. Using this method can yield some surprising results as it brings a creative perspective into our inner life.

Sometimes journals can be used to record dreams (and nightmares). Although dream interpretation can be imprecise, we do know that the unconscious mind utilizes dreaming as a needed mechanism to process emotionally impactful elements. This can include elements that frighten, sadden, and anger us, scenarios that provide us with hope and joy, or experiences that affect us profoundly. Capturing the main points of our dreams immediately after we wake can provide an interesting feedback mechanism and fertile material that helps us to understand what matters most to us. Additionally, keeping our dreams in a journal allows us the opportunity to later contemplate the emotional significance of our dreams.

The ideal journaling method can vary for everyone; however, all religious leaders can benefit from journaling as a useful exercise of emotional self-awareness. Anyone who has been involved in Clinical Pastoral Education (CPE) has had the experience of writing reflections and using them to identify emotional "triggers" or experiences.

SEEKING EXTERNAL PERSPECTIVE

Feedback from others is essential for us to learn the ways in which we need to grow. Many effective avenues exist for seeking honest, objective feedback, including counseling, mentorship, coaching, spiritual direction, and supervision. When we pursue feedback, we must remain open to hearing comments we might be unprepared to receive or acknowledge. This information can include the reactions or perceptions of others to our behavior, tone, and nonverbal language. It's crucial, then, to remember that our desire to develop emotional self-awareness requires us to remain open to all feedback, especially when it elicits a strong reaction in us. "Should you find a wise critic to point out your faults, follow him as you would a guide to hidden treasure."[9]

Counseling

Seeking professional counseling can be one of the best decisions religious leaders can make for themselves. In our work as religious leaders, we have few, if any, confidants who can provide a trustworthy, private, and insightful sounding board. This limits our opportunities for safe self-reflection, so enlisting the help of a professional therapist is advisable. In addition to providing a safe place to share our thoughts and feelings, therapists are trained to recognize the psychological elements of ego and perfectionism that were discussed previously. A therapist may also encourage journaling as a resource for us to understand ourselves better. Professional therapists are required by law to keep our confidences, with rare exceptions that are communicated to clients at the outset of the therapeutic relationship (e.g., reported child abuse). One of the salient features of professional counseling is that therapists are loyal to their clients, not to a church or denomination. This alliance can be quite comforting when circumstances become difficult in our work, and we feel the painful pangs of isolation and loneliness that occur within religious leadership.

Mentors and Coaches

Our emotional self-awareness can also benefit tremendously from mentorship and coaching relationships. A mentor is typically a seasoned religious leader whom we enlist to provide good advice and healthy feedback regarding our vocation. Some denominations assign mentors to new religious leaders or to those who are encountering difficulties in their work. For those who have the opportunity to pick their own mentor, it is helpful to choose someone they admire and trust.

Similarly, coaches are typically professionals who are hired by us, or by our denomination, to assist our professional development. Some coaches are experts in the field of EQ who can actively promote our growth in emotional self-awareness through such tools as temperament testing, 360-degree assessment, and professional workshops. One of the useful testing instruments that some coaches utilize to assess the EQ of pastors is the Social/Emotional Competence Inventory from the Hay Group in Boston. This instrument is a multirater inventory with up to a dozen people who complete the same inventory for each participant. A similar multirater inventory is produced by Multi-Health Systems in Toronto, Ontario.

With these inventories, the test is ordered and administered by credentialed individuals, such as the faith-based professionals at the Center for Emotional Intelligence and Human Relations Skills (EQ-HR), where Roy formerly served as executive director. Their website, http://www.eqhr.org, lists a variety of coaches who use inventories such as those we've just mentioned. These trained professionals can help the participant to interpret and understand the comprehensive test results.

The EQ-HR Center also offers intensive experiential workshops for religious leaders that are designed to move participants into deeper emotional self-awareness and improved effectiveness within their organizations. For example, the Johari Window is a technique developed in 1955[10] to guide the discovery of the differences between our self-perception and the perception of others. It has been used and adapted over the years by psychologists and organizational consultants for the development of individuals and groups toward enhanced work relationships and more effective communication. The EQ-HR Center uses the Johari Window as a technique to help religious leaders become emotionally self-aware and more competent in working with others.

Spiritual Direction

Another resource through which to gain emotional self-awareness can come from engaging a spiritual director. Spiritual directors typically have considerable training in spiritual formation, and can provide an insightful focus upon our spiritual development on a personal level. Just as therapists provide guidance and perception into our emotional and psychological state, spiritual directors can help religious leaders promote understanding and growth within our spiritual selves. United Methodist bishop William Hutchinson explained that clergy who utilize spiritual direction tend to be "less reactionary, less judgmental, more centered, more reflective. They search for deeper answers."[11]

Supervision

We can also gain valuable insight from supervisors during formal training programs, such as that which can occur with Clinical Pastoral Education (CPE), which provides an outstanding opportunity to experience trained supervision as we learn to help people in crisis.[12] With CPE, participants can receive an education that integrates training in theology, psychology, and practical ministry. This formal preparation can help those who serve in congregational work, chaplaincy, or pastoral counseling. The Association for Clinical Pastoral Education, Inc., explained how CPE training could foster the needed trait of emotional self-awareness: "Out of an intense involvement with persons in need, and the feedback from peers and teachers, students develop a new awareness of themselves as persons and of the needs of those to whom they minister."[13]

Having a Mutual Relations Committee (also called Parish Relations Committee) is an informal type of supervision that can help with emotional self-awareness. This is typically a group of four to five trusted congregants who meet regularly, act as an accountability group, and serve as liaisons and advocates between religious leaders and congregants. This group can offer encouragement and guidance while providing a needed filter for complaints. These committee members should never be in dual relationships (e.g., not serving simultaneously on the committee and as a direct supervisor or employee) to prevent bias so we can speak with more candor with the committee members. Preferably, we can pick our own committee members or at least provide a list of people from which the committee can be selected. Perhaps most importantly, this group is invested in our health and success over an extended period and can provide feedback about our behavior and its effects. This committee can provide insights and perspectives that we might not otherwise receive. This increased clarity can greatly improve our emotional self-awareness if we approach these interactions with humility and transparency.

It is ideal if we can share our concerns openly with our mentor, coach, spiritual director, or mutual relations committee without fear of disciplinary action from our supervisors.[14] As mentioned earlier, trust is essential when we receive feedback and guidance. For example, one veteran religious leader referred to the emotional benefit and positive connection they received from their mentorship and coaching relationships as "relational connectivity."

EMOTIONAL SELF-AWARENESS AS A FOUNDATION

In this chapter, we've given you examples of some ways in which you can explore yourself and build your own emotional self-awareness. Developing emotional self-awareness will help you understand a fuller set of reasons you became a religious leader, why you act in the manner you do, and why you react to people in certain ways. You can also learn how to manage your ego, grow past your tendency toward perfectionism, become more resilient, and recognize unhealthy behaviors. Once you realize your need for emotional self-awareness, you can actively develop this pivotal EQ trait by studying temperament theory and by gaining internal and external perspective with the resources we have recommended.

Accepting the challenge to develop emotional self-awareness requires courage. You will find yourself growing and deepening emotionally and spiritually as you continue to expand your EQ. Exploring the unknown can be frightening, and the process of self-discovery can be unsettling and even shocking. We want you to know that this process is worth any discomfort you may feel along the way because it will allow you to realize the entirety of your personality and retain the purity of your calling. Facing this challenge is a worthwhile venture, for as Carl

Jung wrote: "Your visions will become clear only when you can look into your own heart. Who looks outside, dreams; who looks inside, awakes."[15]

4

UTILIZING EMOTIONAL SELF-CONTROL

People can be really aggravating and get me really upset. I've got to pull myself out of the situation most of the time, and reflect and pray. I think it's one of those difficult situations, especially where anger is something I struggle with. When I want to change people through my own strength, I have to realize: "No, no, I can't do that."

—Anonymous pastor

Now that we've addressed the EQ trait of Emotional Self-Awareness, it's important to examine the trait of Emotional Self-Control because the two EQ traits are closely connected. For many of us, it's easy to remember an instance in our personal or professional lives when our emotions got the best of us—a time when we wish we could take back something we said or did in that critical moment. As we learned in the previous chapters, it's not fair to ask ourselves to completely control how our emotions affect us, or to suggest that we can keep ourselves from making any further emotional missteps. Remember, we are perfectly imperfect, and that's okay. However, our emotional self-awareness can be developed, and in so doing, we can avoid the worst of our mistakes that otherwise might happen because of our unchecked feelings and impulses. When we are unable to manage our emotions, our professional competence suffers, and our interpersonal relationships can be damaged.

For the most part, we, the authors, are aware that there will always be powerful emotions playing inside of us. We may not understand where these emotions come from or why they are so intense. When we acquire the trait of Emotional Self-Control, we can take an accurate inventory of our feelings and choose the best course of action. This inventory is much like Stephen King described in *The Gunslinger*: "his way was to . . . consult his own interior, utterly mysterious workings, and then act."[1]

In some cases, emotional self-control is revealed by our ability to tolerate uncertainty as we explore our emotions and the options available to us. Once we understand and find some comfort amidst what we are feeling, the best strategy often reveals itself. Those who manage themselves best are those who can endure difficult situations without losing control of their emotions. Success comes to those who can put their immediate needs on hold and consistently manage their emotional tendencies.

WHAT IS EMOTIONAL SELF-CONTROL?

The trait of Emotional Self-Control can be defined as the ability to manage powerful and disruptive feelings and to prevent those emotions from damaging our professional and personal lives. If emotional self-awareness provides us the ability to read our own emotions effectively and to recognize their impact, then emotional self-control gives us the ability to manage our words and actions during emotional situations. In other words, once we recognize what we are feeling, can we act and react to these stimuli in a healthy and productive manner? As Adele Lynn explained: "If I have some awareness and self-understanding, then I can ask: what is my impact on others, in my current state? If I find that impact to be negative—if I find that it detracts from my life goals—I may choose to change my actions, thoughts or words."[2]

A double-sided risk exists for us when we experience negative emotions. On the one hand, we can "act out" emotions in negative ways, such as exploding with anger and suffering the consequences. On the other hand, we can ignore and suppress our negative emotions and pretend they are insignificant. When we do this, psychological defense mechanisms such as denial, repression, sublimation, and projection can occur with significantly negative results. This double threat is a unique challenge for religious leaders because we often feel pressure to hide our negative feelings from others to show that we have achieved a higher level of spirituality. The specific mechanics of these threats and the powerful psychological functions involved within them are discussed later in this chapter. We also explain what healthy emotional self-control looks like for religious leaders.

Emotional self-control should neither serve as a method for stifling our emotions, nor as an excuse to allow our emotions to operate in an unrestrained way. It's helpful to think of our feelings as a powerful energy source that can be channeled and harnessed for good. For example, in 1896 Nicholas Tesla successfully harnessed the power of Niagara Falls for electricity in New York City.[3] Our emotions are much like that huge waterfall—beautiful and powerful, yet beyond our complete mastery. We can neither stifle nor prevent ourselves from having feelings any more than we can stop the flow of Niagara Falls. At the same time, we can't allow our feelings to flow uncontrolled without causing significant damage. Therefore, self-control is the healthy balance between constrained (stifled) and unrestrained emotion (figure 4.1). Later in this chapter, we discuss practical ways for religious leaders to maintain this balance.

SPIRITUAL AND PHILOSOPHICAL BASIS OF EMOTIONAL SELF-CONTROL

Emotional self-control has strong spiritual and philosophical roots. For example, Buddhist philosophy asserts that attachments and desire are the cause of all suffering (dissatisfaction) and pain. Whenever we become attached strongly to something, we grasp it tightly and stake our future on possessing whatever we desire. Examples of this can include money, a good job, a relationship, a house, a new car, our health, our youthful looks, our kids turning out a certain way—or anything in the world to which we pin our happiness. When it doesn't turn out that way, we become depressed or angry and increase the risk of dwelling in an increasingly negative emotional state. However, we can reduce our emotional discomfort by learning to accept our life in its current condition, specifically those circumstances over which we have no control or influence. In other words, we can increase our emotional self-control with a sound spiritual approach that minimizes our negative emotions.

Figure 4.1.   The Balance between Constrained and Unrestrained Emotion

We can also learn from the practice of mindfulness when sharpening our skills of emotional self-control.[4] One of the main tenets of mindfulness teaches us to be aware of our emotions and how they affect our body. For example, Daniel Goleman explained how emotionally difficult situations could stimulate our amygdala, which is commonly understood as the source in our brain of our fight-or-flight reflex.[5] Without the full resources of our brain at work to analyze various inputs, the amygdala often makes sloppy mistakes because the dangers it faces are symbolic, not physical threats. As a result, this causes us to lose the emotional self-control needed for effective interpersonal communication and wise decision making. It's as if the amygdala has hijacked the rest of our brain and we go into survival mode. However, with mindfulness, we learn to identify when we are having a visceral reaction by noticing the different sensations that occur in our body. For instance, our muscles may become tense, or we may begin to clench our teeth.

These physical sensations can serve as useful signals that tell us we need to implement methods of self-soothing. We cover some of these methods later in this chapter.

Christian teaching further illuminates the concept of emotional self-control, for even Jesus showed his emotions, including negative feelings. For instance, he experienced strong anger (showing his wrath with the moneychangers in the temple), profound sadness (weeping when Lazarus died), intense anguish (beseeching, "Father, why have you forsaken me?"), supreme dread (pleading with God to forego his imminent torture and execution), and stark betrayal (experiencing Judas's kiss). These examples help us understand that it's okay for us to feel negative emotions, just as Jesus did.

If we're not careful, we can mistake spirituality for an unemotional, undemonstrative, and stoic visage that masks our feelings and suppresses our authentic reactions. In contrast, Christian precepts teach us to recognize our emotions as valid and to react responsibly to them. For instance, Ephesians 4:26 admonishes us "in your anger, do not sin." Also, Jesus recognized the validity of grief and sadness when he said: "Blessed are they who mourn, for they will be comforted" (Matthew 5:4). It's important to remember that the principles of Christianity do not preempt the necessity of our humanity. Ultimately, we are emotional beings who must learn to recognize and manage our feelings, regardless of the depth of our spirituality.

CONTROLLING STRONG EMOTIONS

The highly charged emotional nature of working in religious settings can provoke us into intense emotional reactions. For example, if we are accused of incompetence or laziness, we sometimes believe we are failing in our call of service to God. For many of us, these types of confrontations affect us profoundly, so it takes uncommon emotional maturity and skill in emotional self-control to address such conflicts. Eleanor Roosevelt emphasized the importance of exercising emotional intelligence amid conflict: "When handling yourself, use your head; to handle others, use your heart."[6]

Aside from facing conflict, we sometimes encounter other difficult emotional scenarios in religious leadership. For example, we face grief when others experience tragedy. As religious leaders, we share their sadness and tears in these situations, just as a family member would. Another example of facing difficult situations occurs when we help families overcome relationship challenges, such as with the volatile conflict that can occur for married couples, or the intense struggle that sometimes happens between parents and their teenage children. In these instances, others can feel much better because of our efforts to support them; however, we can become emotionally exhausted from these experiences. As a result of working amid other's feelings, our own emotional state can become quite brittle. We can't expect ourselves to continually serve others without experiencing an accumulation of stress, grief, anger, frustration, or despair, so we must exercise emotional self-control to survive.

Negative emotions are not the only strong feelings that warrant caution. For example, we sometimes experience an emotional "high" after a well-delivered sermon, or when a particularly powerful interpersonal connection occurs with someone. However, this feeling of elation is much like the basic phenomenon of gravity: what comes up, must come down. Because of this, many of us have experienced powerful discouragement or depression in the hours or days that follow these positively charged times. Emotional self-control can help us to regulate our emotional responses to the powerful stimuli that occur when working with people. We can learn to keep our feelings from spiking too high or from plummeting too low.

Even positive emotions can hurt others if acted upon without restraint. For example, if we become too pleased with our performance, status, good fortune, or spiritual growth, we can begin to act arrogantly or to speak boastfully. As religious leaders, this attitude can trample the feelings of others who are struggling and who need encouragement. Our unwitting message to these people is that their lives do not measure up favorably to ours. Our blessings should not be used as an incidental weapon against others.

We can be guilty of disguising prideful messages as false humility. This practice occurs more often than we'd like to admit. If we aren't careful, we can become masters of the "humblebrag."[7] A good example of humblebragging from a pastor is: "I feel so humbled and blessed by how many people have rededicated their lives to God this month." As religious leaders, we mustn't allow ourselves to become boastful, or our service will become tainted. Imagine if Jesus posted on social media: "That moment when you're washing the disciples' feet, and you start an argument with Peter. Epic Fail!" We can still celebrate our successes without bragging; we simply need to consistently give proper credit to others for their service, and the ultimate glory to God. Jesus said: "Why do you call me good? No one is good—except God alone" (Mark 10:18).

As previously discussed, it is true humility that prevents us from acting carelessly or without considering the feelings of others. If we want to prevent unnecessary harm from coming to others or to our relationships, emotional self-control must preside over the full spectrum of our feelings.

WHAT EMOTIONAL SELF-CONTROL IS *NOT*

As mentioned earlier, we can easily confuse emotional self-control with psychological defense mechanisms such as denial, repression, sublimation, and projection. In other words, we may mistakenly believe we are exercising proper self-control over our emotions because we don't allow ourselves to express emotion to anyone, even ourselves. However, failing to learn the difference between healthy emotional self-control and maladaptive psychological tendencies can be harmful. Our emotions are powerful forces that must be accounted for, just as we must plan for a power surge in our home in the event of a lightning strike. Simply pretending that our emotional energy is nonexistent or irrelevant is a dangerous approach. Ultimately, we are emotional creatures working among emotional people in emotionally charged situations.

Many of us find we are not prepared to address the emotional intensity inherent in religious leadership. During our formal training, we typically learned theology and developed our spirituality, and both are key elements of our work. However, after first experiencing the emotional kaleidoscope that comes with religious leadership, many of us discover that these elements alone are inadequate when it comes to dealing with the emotional challenges that arise.

Because of our limited preparation in EQ, our instinct is to unconsciously employ one or more of the defense mechanisms described below to protect ourselves. Without training, coaching, or therapy, we are usually unaware that these psychological devices have been brought to bear in our lives. By becoming aware of these devices, we can learn to implement emotional self-control as a healthy alternative to psychological defense mechanisms when facing significant emotional stressors.

Denial

When an emotionally stressful situation arises, one of our first reactions can be to deny that a problem exists. For example, a pastor might be unable to admit that many members in their church have begun to disagree with their vision as a leader. As a result, they are unaware that their job security has become fragile. The pastor is then caught completely off guard when the board calls them into a meeting to explain: "We've decided to go in a different direction," thus unceremoniously ending the leader's employment. In these cases, we often wonder how we missed the key signs that a change was imminent. Learning how to overcome denial is a vital step toward avoiding such an unfortunate outcome.

A religious leader may also be unable to admit to being poorly suited for his or her current role due to a mismatch in temperament type and duties of the position (described in chapter 3). In these instances, such individuals work harder and harder to find success in their current job, instead of realizing they should find a role more suitable for their gifts. Other religious leaders may need to take a long break from the ministry, but are unable to admit to themselves that they are desperately in need of change. In this context, denial can be understood as an inability for us to recognize and interpret our emotional landscape. With the combination of emotional self-awareness and emotional self-control, however, we learn to identify feelings such as futility, discouragement, and exhaustion in sufficient time for us to intervene effectively on our own behalf.

Repression

Like denial, repression takes place for us when we bury painful emotions instead of finding healthy expression for our feelings. One example of this can occur when a religious leader or counselor loses a congregant or client to suicide. The shock and intense pain associated with such a loss can be so extreme that we unconsciously set these powerful emotions aside. Unfortunately, this can be dangerous because intense emotional experiences demand a healthy release. When feelings of this magnitude are stuffed down, they can cause significant disruption in our lives. As a result, we lose the ability to accurately identify and regulate our feelings because our perspective and judgment become distorted.

Our work requires emotional clarity because we continually interact with people and their feelings. Unfortunately, repression creates a dangerous cocktail of unresolved inner turmoil combined with the ongoing emotional situations of others. Left unchecked, repression can lead to self-destructive behavior, such as alcoholism, substance abuse, overeating, gambling, pornography, and extramarital affairs. The answer to this problem can be as simple as sharing our struggles with a trusted confidant. Emotional self-control allows us to reach out for help when we are in pain, rather than ignore it until our emotional wounds turn septic. As Paul Stevens wrote: "It is sad to admit, but many pastors turn to alcohol and/or drug abuse, or some other damaging behavior as a way of unwinding from the stress of ministry. That is why it is crucial to have someone to talk to and be yourself."[8]

Sublimation

Sublimation is a somewhat less destructive defense mechanism in which we unconsciously transform socially unacceptable emotional impulses into socially acceptable behavior. This mechanism is one in which religious leaders are particularly susceptible because we are under constant pressure to be "good" people. For example, pastors who are lonely might visit their church members quite frequently without realizing they are attempting to meet their own social needs.

Another example of sublimation is the pastor who mows the church lawn because cutting the grass produces a satisfying sense of completion. What we may not realize is that we often take on extra tasks because it feels good to get something done. These tasks provide a nice contrast to our ongoing and unfinished work with people.

Through sublimation, we can turn our uncomfortable feelings into behavior that is less destructive than denial or repression. However, we should be aware of the risks involved when we utilize sublimation because the nature of our work makes setting boundaries difficult. In other words, once we have added activities to our long list of duties, it's almost impossible to remove them. Once we start doing these "extras," some people expect us to continue doing them long after these activities no longer provide comfort to us. Because of this, we need to examine how we spend our time and be cautious about making new commitments.

Because of our desire to be "good," combined with the extensive expectations of others, one of the biggest risks for those of us who are prone to sublimation is the tendency to become workaholics. Without a safe and healthy outlet for our emotions, a perfect storm occurs that can lead to a dangerous and addictive pattern of overachievement. However, this danger can be avoided through emotional self-control because it allows us the means to address our feelings of discouragement, disappointment, frustration, and anxiety before we work ourselves to death.

Projection

Projection occurs when we unconsciously attribute our emotional impulses to others. This mechanism manifests itself in a unique and dangerous way for religious leaders due to the high level of influence we have over others. For example, a preacher who struggles with frustration due to being unable to find healthy sexual expression might preach consistently about sexual immorality. Another religious leader who worries excessively about money may overemphasize the necessity of tithing. Yet another example is the minister who battles feelings of abandonment and so insists upon perfect church attendance.

In addition to communicating from the pulpit, projection can occur for religious leaders in their interpersonal communication. For example, a religious leader who feels unworthy of their position may hold staff and volunteers to impossible standards. With emotional awareness and self-control, religious leaders can address their emotional pitfalls in a cognizant and responsible manner.

PRACTICAL WAYS TO DEVELOP EMOTIONAL SELF-CONTROL

Recognize Triggers

One of the paramount ways to develop emotional self-control is to learn to recognize our triggers. A trigger occurs when a certain circumstance activates strong emotions within us. Triggers are based upon previous painful experiences, and so we often react defensively when we are consciously or unconsciously reminded of a particular occurrence. For example, we might encounter someone who speaks us in the same negative way that a family member once did (or continues to do). We may or may not be aware that we are triggered by this type of communication style. In such instances, our emotional reaction under these circumstances can be harmful to that relationship.

Ideally, we should be able to heal from prior emotional and spiritual injuries. However, this can be an unrealistic expectation because healing typically happens over time. Many wounds remain tender to the "touch" long after they have healed and scarred over. Learning to identify our triggers and recognize then they occur is a significant first step toward emotional self-control. Without this self-knowledge, we tend to react to our triggers with no awareness or emotional regulation. However, emotional self-control allows us to safely manage our emotional impulses when triggers occur.

Find a Safe Place to Express Emotions

In some instances, it behooves us to honestly express our emotions even after we have identified them. This is a principal step in the process of emotional self-control because it provides the safe outlet or release needed for us to process our feelings properly. In contrast, feelings that are expressed irresponsibly can be damaging. For instance, yelling or cursing at someone when we are angry can shatter the relationship. Instead, we need to find a way to express our feelings that will lead to catharsis, but limits the destruction to our relationships and career. For example, we might meet one-on-one with a coworker with whom we have a conflict and explain that we are frustrated or angry with that person, and why we feel this way (Matthew 18:15–17). In this scenario, we allow the coworker to express him- or herself honestly and preserve the coworker's dignity. This allows our emotional energy to flow while preserving or improving our relationship with the coworker. In so doing, we can "let go" of the emotions that cause us discomfort and move on from the difficult circumstance without resentment.

Not all our feelings can be safely expressed within our religious organization. In these instances, it may be best to express our feelings to a professional therapist or coach. As discussed in chapter 3, these professionals can be trustworthy guides for us as we sort through our emotions. For example, we can tell a therapist when we suffer doubts about our professional abilities without risking a loss of the confidence of others in our organization. Similarly, as suggested in chapter 3, journaling regularly can be a safe outlet for emotional issues.

Establish Emotional Boundaries

The concept of boundaries can be understood and utilized in multiple ways. First, emotional energy can be thought of as a limited resource that requires careful budgeting. Therefore, we shouldn't waste our energy on those people or situations that tend to drain us unnecessarily. Nathan DeWall called this becoming a "mental energy accountant."[9] We can set healthy external boundaries by avoiding those difficult situations that can be avoided, such as not engaging in unnecessary arguments. With emotional self-control, we can detect those individuals who love conflict and choose to forego a debate with them. As the saying goes: "Whoever argues with a fool becomes a fool."

Also worth consideration is the practice of setting internal boundaries. When utilized correctly, internal boundaries can prevent our emotions from escalating or descending to dangerous levels. For example, when we feel ourselves slipping into despair, we can call a close friend, trusted family member, or mentor to remind ourselves that we are not alone. Similarly, if we find that our anxiety is climbing to an uncomfortable level, we can read our favorite book or scriptural passage. Additionally, when we suffer from discontent, we can spend time helping others with problems worse than our own. Furthermore, when we get angry, we can stop to meditate and pray to find our center and sense of peace. As Jane Austen wrote in *Sense and Sensibility*: "I will be calm. I will be mistress of myself."[10] Although we can't fully control our emotions, we can learn to manage them through effective internal boundary setting.

Maintain Consistent Self-Care

Because ministry work revolves around serving the needs of others, it's easy for us to neglect our own needs. For example, a hospital chaplain might spend an entire shift working with a bereaved family and later realize he or she hasn't eaten all day. Similarly, a youth pastor or counselor might spend the night working with a suicidal adolescent and then continue working the next day without sleep. When we neglect our self-care (e.g., food, emotional and physical rest, medical care, mental health), we create an untenable deficit within our physical and emotional system. In other words, we have no emotional energy left for ourselves or for others. When this happens, we can become irritable, maudlin, or hypervigilant. Therefore, it's important to recognize our responsibility to self-advocate and make sure our needs are consistently met.

Physical self-care can be maintained through surprisingly simple decisions. For example, we can learn to take small breaks throughout our workday to limit fatigue. We can also consistently take a daily lunch break, so that we remain nourished and rested. We might also consult with a doctor, nutritionist, or personal trainer about the best types of food, drink, and supplements needed to maintain good health. Additionally, many religious leaders find that exercising for twenty to thirty minutes during their lunch hour provides an invaluable release from their daily stress. Finally, taking a proper annual vacation can do wonders for recharging our physical and emotional health. Even periodic two-day getaways can be renewing.

Learning to breathe properly can also be an amazing resource to keep us healthy during times of stress. Oftentimes, when under duress, our breathing becomes shallow or we hold our breath without knowing it, so it's important for us to become aware of such tendencies. Taking a yoga class can offer valuable training in deep breathing and focused movement. One example of religious leaders who experience a great deal of emotional stress is hospice chaplains, who often travel from one place to another to meet with dying patients and their families, offering support and comfort. For them, renewal can be gained by stopping near a park between home visits just to walk and breathe.

Like physical self-care, our emotional self-care is also maintained through a series of choices. For example, we can develop or maintain a social support system outside of our work setting, whether that be with family, friends, or both. This choice encourages and allows us to have a balanced life that does not revolve around our work. We can also practice healthy self-soothing during times of stress or anguish, such as listening to our favorite music, watching an entertaining show, or looking at photos that comfort us. Sometimes taking the time to watch a sunrise or sunset can also improve our perspective.

Many of us make excuses to keep from maintaining our self-care, such as the intense demands of our work, the high expectations of our organization, or our "hard-charging" personality. Please hear this: these excuses for poor self-care do not originate from our spirituality (i.e., from God), but rather from our emotional selves. Otherwise stated, without self-care, our desire to succeed, fear of failure or rejection, anxiety about the future, and other deep-seated feelings will push us past our human endurance. Jesus himself stated that his "yoke is easy and his burden is light" (Matthew 11:28–30). Once we learn to maintain consistent self-care, it's surprising to discover how much of our professional burden has been a result of our own choices. Once we learn to take proper care of ourselves, emotional self-control becomes much easier because we are at full strength.

Exercise Good Judgment

One of the qualities we can learn during the development of spiritual leadership can be the exercise of good judgment during emotionally charged situations. For example, good judgment can be shown by keeping a clear head when others are upset or angry. As Proverbs 15:1 teaches: "A soft answer turns away wrath." If we allow our emotions to take over our judgment, we miss the opportunity to defuse difficult scenarios and set a good example for others. Bohdi Sanders aptly described this approach: "Never respond to an angry person with a fiery comeback, even if the person deserves it. . . . Don't allow [their] anger to become your anger."[11]

Good judgment can also keep us from jumping to incorrect conclusions, especially regarding the motivations of others. In other words, we can easily assume the worst intentions from others during times of misunderstanding and conflict. With emotional self-control, we learn to discuss matters maturely before resentment sets in and our relationships become ruined. With good judgment, we learn how to balance our logical mind with our powerful feelings so that we can make wise decisions.

MOVING FROM UNDERSTANDING OURSELVES TO EMPATHY

Each of us (the authors) has vivid memories of some of the negative consequences we experienced before we began our work to develop emotional self-control. We remember the feelings of embarrassment, humiliation, sadness, and regret (to name a few) that were part of the aftermath of our poor judgment or hasty reactions. While they are difficult memories, we can acknowledge their role in our development. The challenge for us is the same as it is for every religious leader: we must consistently practice emotional self-control lest our emotions result in damaging behaviors. In our humanness, there are still times when our emotions and defense mechanisms take over, and we find ourselves living with the consequences of our actions. The good news is that our understanding of the behaviors of others can deepen when we learn to understand and accept our own shortcomings. In the next chapter, you will discover how to transform your growing self-knowledge into the powerful skill of empathy for others.

5

GAINING EMPATHY

*I do not ask the wounded person how he feels, I myself become the
wounded person.*

—Walt Whitman[1]

Have you ever had the experience of listening to someone who is in
pain, or is angry and frustrated? And, at any of those times, have you
found yourself *feeling* that person's pain, anger, or frustration? Did that
allow you to respond more compassionately and without judgment, simply accepting the person's experience as real? If so, you have known
empathy. You have walked inside someone's experience and connected
with that person. These moments are, indeed, holy moments!

In the previous chapter, we established the need for religious leaders to develop emotional self-control. Now we will explore the trait of
Empathy and why it is so crucial to our religious leadership. Daniel
Goleman wrote that emotional self-control is directly tied to empathy,[2]
a significant connection for us to recognize. If we don't understand
ourselves and why we behave in certain ways, we will not be able to
understand the motivations and behaviors of others.

We need empathy to understand those we serve and to comprehend
why they act as they do. It's much easier to keep from losing our temper
or from holding a grudge if we learn to understand their point of view.
One pastor explained that understanding the people in his church
helped him to step back, and kept him from punching holes in walls due
to the powerful frustrations he felt from religious leadership. More
significantly, empathy helps us to better serve others by showing that

we genuinely care about them. In so doing, we act as agents of comfort and healing during their darkest moments. Audrey Hepburn explained her belief in the importance of empathy by proclaiming: "Nothing is more important than empathy for another person's suffering."[3]

For some of us, utilizing empathy is a new and difficult skill to learn. Others of us are naturally empathic, yet we struggle with keeping healthy boundaries. In the following sections, we will discuss the EQ concept of empathy, how to develop it, and how and when to show it to others.

WHAT IS EMPATHY?

As religious leaders, we are frequently asked to help others with their problems, frustrations, and pain. Empathy is the skill that allows us to connect with people on an emotional level. It requires us to invest our heart into their lives and to reassure them that they are not alone. The trait of Empathy is best understood in three parts: "*knowing* another person's feelings, *feeling* what that person feels, and *responding* compassionately to another person's distress."[4]

Empathy may be the subtlest of all the EQ traits because it is a passive skill. It asks us to be emotionally present with others in their pain, instead of jumping into action to fix their problems. Because of this, empathy can best be understood as a state of being rather than a set of activities or interventions. People sometimes describe an empathic person as someone who is "there for them." Homer offered a good description of empathy: "Taught by time, my heart has learned to glow for other's good, and melt at other's woe."[5]

Empathy is not sympathy. Sympathy is when we feel sorry for someone or show pity for them, which strips them of their unique human dignity.[6] In contrast, empathy requires that we respect a person enough to listen and do our best to comprehend their perspective. As one pastor explained: "I step back and try to put myself in their shoes." This approach allows us to come beside them and show that we understand that they are hurting. By allowing ourselves to share someone's pain, we validate that person's existence as a feeling person. We have the power to show people that it's okay to have feelings and trust themselves. It can also give them hope that things can get better.

SHOWING EMPATHY CAN BE CHALLENGING

Empathy can be a difficult skill for us to learn because we often feel as though we are expected to be problem-solvers for others—especially when they ask us for help and guidance. In these situations, we typically offer our best advice and theological counsel. However, there are key moments when people merely need for us to listen and care about them. A key to empathy is simply to help others feel heard and understood.

As religious leaders, it can be difficult to refrain from judging others when they share their dark secrets, because part of our role includes preaching and teaching morality to others. As such, we sometimes think of ourselves as spiritual police officers or as guardians of truth. When people share things that violate our sensibilities, is it more important for us to set them straight, or to help them heal?

Jesus demonstrated the answer when he addressed the woman caught in adultery: "Neither do I condemn you. Now go and sin no more" (John 8:11b, BSB). First, Jesus helped the woman to heal; then he taught her how to grow from the situation. Consider the contrast between the men who were preparing to stone her for adultery and Jesus who chose not to condemn her. In fact, the men walked away after Jesus reminded them of their own imperfections. Empathy allows us to go beyond the habitual judgment of behaviors that we consider to be immoral.

Our ego can also influence us toward judgment, with internal commentary such as: "Well, at least I've never done that." Brené Brown explained how our judgments can come from a place of insecurity:

> Empathy is incompatible with shame and judgment. Staying out of judgment requires understanding. We tend to judge those areas where we're the most vulnerable to feeling shame ourselves. We don't tend to judge others in areas where our sense of self-worth is stable and secure. In order to stay out of judgment, we must pay attention to our own triggers and issues.[7]

Marcus Aurelius also addressed how we can be prone to judgment: "Whenever you are about to find fault with someone, ask yourself the following question: What fault of mine most nearly resembles the one I am about to criticize?"[8] Fortunately, our previous work with emotional self-awareness in chapters 2 and 3 can be very helpful in preventing us from turning to judgment instead of empathy. It also helps when we remember Jesus's admonition: "Judge not, lest ye be judged" (Matthew 7:1).

THE NEED FOR EMPATHY AS RELIGIOUS LEADERS

Those who come to us for help need us to show empathy for so many reasons. As mentioned earlier, people need us to be empathic when they are hurting. When we are, we can provide a place where they find safe harbor during their life's storm, especially when they have nowhere else to turn. Many times, people feel ashamed, worthless, and unlovable. With an empathic attitude and approach, we can model God's love for each person, and teach each of them to appreciate who they are as a divinely and wonderfully created human being (Psalm 139:14). We can think of each person as a stained-glass window that is broken, beautiful, and fully unique, because glass never fragments the same way twice. Therefore, when we show empathy toward others, we share in the privilege of caretaking God's artistry.

Those with whom we work also need us to demonstrate empathy when they make mistakes, especially when serving within our organization. For example, some people get in "over their head" during their volunteer work and they need us to encourage them. One religious leader explained how a congregant was overwhelmed while leading a children's ministry with local neighborhood kids:

> Unless you've worked here . . . it's hard to describe. They steal, they break stuff, they purposefully hurt each other, and they fight like it's a gong show. You know, he had his plan, and he wanted to teach them about Jesus. But all he was doing was being a police officer all night, and he wasn't doing it very well because the group got away from him. I had to come down a bunch of times to help him, and then he felt bad. He was in tears at the end of the day.

We can demonstrate kindness and humility in these situations by sharing the mistakes or shortcomings we made when we were less experienced. We can also coach them to improve in a way that does not crush their spirit. The same interviewee shared how they helped their congregant by asking: "How can we learn from tonight, so when it happens again we are more prepared?"

In times when others share or confess their moral and spiritual failures to us, it is so important that we treat them with compassion and dignity. If we are not careful, we can exacerbate their feelings of shame, which can be deeply destructive. Showing empathy in these instances is critical, because people are at high risk of associating condemnation with God if they feel judged by their religious leader.

PRACTICAL WAYS TO GAIN EMPATHY

One of the best ways for us to acquire the trait of Empathy is to learn how to listen deeply. Like any other skill, listening is something we can learn to do effectively through training and practice. When we listen properly to someone, we give that person a rare gift. The person may feel heard for the first time in a long while, if not for the very first time. Hearing someone's story without interruption, distraction, or judgment is the first step toward demonstrating empathy. M. Scott Peck wrote: "The most important form of attention we can give our loved ones is listening. . . . True listening is love in action."9

Most professional counselors learn to become active listeners as part of their formal training process. Active listening can be very helpful to religious leaders as well. This process includes several key elements that we can learn as we sharpen our listening skills. First, active listening includes asking open questions so that others are encouraged to share their stories and feelings without interference from us (e.g., "tell me more about . . ."). Second, we can facilitate the conversation by providing "minimal encouragers," such as using the phrase "mm-hmm," or nodding our head at key points in their stories. Next, we can reflect back to them with paraphrasing and summarizing to confirm that we've been listening. This also creates an opportunity to clarify anything we've misunderstood.

We can further demonstrate active listening by maintaining eye contact throughout the conversation to show we are giving our full attention (e.g., not glancing at our phones, watches, computers, or people walking by). Finally, we can demonstrate nonjudgmental and nonthreatening body language, such as leaning forward in our chair to show our interest. This contrasts with body language that doesn't encourage them to keep talking, such as leaning back in our chair with our arms crossed, or propping our head up with our hand, as if we are bored. Overall, the essential elements of becoming a good listener are sincerely wanting to hear what someone else says and giving them our full attention.

In addition to increasing our listening skills, we can also develop empathy by learning how to recognize and interpret nonverbal behavior. Nonverbal behavior can include gestures, body movements, and facial expressions. One religious leader described how they noticed their congregant was troubled by something: "I saw it on her face. I could just read it." We need to enhance our ability to understand the different ways that people communicate with us if we want to understand them fully. Active listening leads to empathy, and empathy can lead to insights about others that we can use to further help them.

RISKS OF EMPATHY FOR RELIGIOUS LEADERS

Like many people who pursue careers in the helping professions, religious leaders tend to be caring and empathic people. Ron Cook wrote that most pastors "are wired with the altruistic mindset. It is that unselfishness for, or devotion to, the welfare of others that is one of the most endearing attributes a pastor brings to a church. They care. They care often and deeply."[10] Because of our deep devotion to our ministry, it's vital that we learn to exercise caution about the people to whom we offer empathy and when we provide it. There are reasons for this. First, some people will take advantage of our time and emotional energy. It is understood that others will go through difficult seasons in their lives that warrant more empathy than at other times. However, some people consistently demand a disproportionate amount of our emotional energy due to their emotional or spiritual immaturity, or in some cases because they have a psychological disorder. While we want to help everyone, we need to be careful when working with some people because they can pull us into the "rabbit hole" of their lives, leaving no time or energy for other individuals, our families, or ourselves.

Additionally, the sheer number of people we serve, and the magnitude of their needs, may exceed our ability to demonstrate empathy for every person, every day. Otherwise stated, the emotional energy required to show empathy is not a limitless resource. In spite of this, many of us will still attempt to test ourselves past the limits of our strength. Cook described how showing empathy could create Empathy Fatigue if we don't maintain emotional and spiritual balance:

> Empathy Fatigue is a pastor's kryptonite. One of the inescapable responsibilities of being a pastor is being "high touch;" much of what we do requires listening and being emotionally involved with people's problems and then responding in truth and love. Empathy Fatigue drains a pastor of their strength when they stubbornly refuse to care for themselves spiritually, emotionally, and physically in the way they tell others to care for themselves. . . . Empathy Fatigue seems to be a black hole, draining us far quicker than we can manage to get our spiritual equilibrium under control.[11]

To counteract Empathy Fatigue, many religious leaders delegate some of the emotional situations they encounter to their staff or co-workers. Still others train lay leaders to help with these circumstances. Some religious leaders also select a trusted professional therapist to whom they can refer others in especially difficult situations.

Perhaps most importantly, we can also learn to release the emotional burdens of others, as well as our own, to God. Remember: God's capacity to care about the problems and pain of humans is much greater than ours.

EMPATHY FOR OUR FAMILY

We often become so fully invested in the lives of those we serve that our work consumes us. However, we must remember that our family needs us to show empathy for them, too. In fact, our family should receive the best of our emotional energy because we are irreplaceable to them. Our ego may believe that no one can take care of others as well as we do, but that is not true. Forgetting this truth is one of the easiest ways for us to lose our work-life balance, which can damage the relationships that matter most. As one interviewee stated: "I've seen too many pastors essentially sacrifice their family for church." Simply stated, our spouses and children do not deserve to be neglected because of our calling. Pastor Scott Thomas described how easily this can happen:

> My initial experiences of success drove me further into pursuing an elusive goal, and I worked countless hours at the expense of my marriage. I reasoned that my loving wife would understand. At first, I justified working long hours by telling myself it would increase the attendance of the church to the point where its offering would sustain the church expenses. But after that was accomplished, I continued to work hard to satisfy my own ego and pride and to gain recognition.[12]

If we believe we should show empathy toward those we serve, we must remember that providing empathy for our family members is twice as important. Sometimes this can be as simple as hearing them when they have something meaningful to share with us. One religious leader said: "When I carry all of the wackiness of pain and hurt into my family life, my wife gets overwhelmed. How do I know? She tells me."

Our family and friends will be in our lives long after our religious leadership ends, especially if we showed empathy to them when they needed us. A strong word of advice: our primary ministry should always be to our family. When we pay attention to our family's needs, our home life becomes balanced because our priorities are properly aligned. This, in turn, can help us to better serve others because we have more emotional energy to give.

A CALL FOR COMPASSION

Developing empathy comes easier for some religious leaders than it does for others. The ease with which we develop and deepen our capacity to empathize is dependent upon our ability to open our heart and experience an emotional and spiritual connection with others. Otherwise, we are in danger of staying hidden inside the armor of our own ego. When we move beyond our ego into empathy, we can accept that people live their lives with the best intentions, whatever that means to each of us and no matter how flawed we may be. Meister Eckhart, a theologian who wrote extensively about compassion, declared: "You need to love all persons as yourself, esteeming them and considering them alike. What happens to another, *whether it be a joy or a sorrow,* happens to you."[13]

When we suspend judgment, and avoid the temptation to assume we know the intentions of others, we are then ready to use our knowledge and skills to improve our effectiveness as we work with entire congregations, organizations, and communities. The next chapter focuses on the trait of Organizational Awareness. As you have most likely learned, working within an organization brings rewards and challenges that are very different from those we encounter when working with individuals. We can further hone our leadership by gaining insight into organizational dynamics. In so doing, we can learn how to anticipate and respond to these forces with poise and confidence.

6

LEARNING ORGANIZATIONAL AWARENESS

Organizational effectiveness does not lie in that narrow-minded concept called rationality. It lies in the blend of clearheaded logic and powerful intuition.

—Henry Mintzberg[1]

In the last chapter, we addressed how to develop empathy, which is an important step toward developing the EQ trait of Organizational Awareness. As we learn to listen to people better, we begin to understand each of them and their points of view. When we understand the individuals in our organization, we can then begin to gain an awareness of their collective emotional state. Organizational awareness involves comprehending people as they operate within a group, and how their various interactions affect one another and the group dynamic. As you read this chapter, you will notice that we have begun to make a significant shift from a focus on your internal perspective toward a more practical, external set of skills.

WHAT IS ORGANIZATIONAL AWARENESS?

Many of the religious leaders we interviewed expressed how valuable it is that they understand the emotional flow of their organization. This process can be an eye-opening experience for newly graduated religious leaders. Many believe that working in a religious organization will be a haven from emotional turmoil or challenges to their professional goals. When we begin our religious leadership, we soon realize how challenging it can be to lead a church or religious organization. This difficulty can materialize within our team of coworkers or with congregants.

What can also be confusing for many religious leaders is how the emotional tenor of our organization can change in ways we did not expect. This confusion happens when we are unaware of who the key stakeholders are in the group and how to communicate with them. These are the individuals in our organization who have considerable sway in shaping programs or policies. We must take account of them if we aim to be successful. The trait of Organizational Awareness is defined as "reading a group's emotional currents and power relationships."[2] In this chapter, we discuss how to view our work as religious leaders in different ways so that our organizational awareness is elevated. We also share practical methods to enhance and utilize this key EQ trait.

RELIGIOUS ORGANIZATIONS ARE NOT FAMILIES

Our family of origin is our first experience within a community. How each of us experienced family, and how those experiences affect our need for community, varies for each of us. For those of us whose family of origin may not have provided for our emotional needs as children, we tend to seek out a group that gives us what we missed in our childhood. Unconsciously, our goal can be to create a surrogate family. This perception can be confusing in religious leadership because there is often a spiritual kinship among those in our church or religious group. For example, many of us commonly use phrases such as "church family" and our "brothers and sisters in God." The realization that our religious organization is not an actual family can be a painful loss of naiveté. We begin to understand that the organization is a poor parent and that this work isn't nearly as safe as we had hoped it would be.

It helps to recognize that religious leadership is our job. This work life can't be counted on to fill our emotional deficits or to help us to heal from past familial wounds. The relationships we build with others can be wonderful and satisfying, but our work can only address some of our desire for community. As discussed earlier, people have their own emotional needs, and this limits their ability to meet ours. To complicate matters, most positions in religious leadership typically last just a few years before we choose to leave or are asked to leave. If we allow ourselves to think of work as our family, we can feel bereft and even abandoned when we are no longer part of that group.

Because our need for community cannot be fully met by those we serve, we need to be part of a community that exists outside of our religious organization. This advice may seem counterintuitive; however, having a support system outside of our work provides the stability we need during the ups and downs of religious leadership. It helps us to survive emotionally and spiritually no matter what happens during our career. Also, having trusted relationships outside of our congregation provides us with needed objectivity and perspective as we address the needs of those we serve and of the religious organization as a whole.

ORGANIZATIONS ARE SYSTEMS

Increasing awareness of our religious organization as a system provides us with a valuable comprehension of how it works. With systems theory, we learn that a system is greater than the sum of its parts. In other words, our organization is more than a random collection of individuals. Rather, the various interactions that occur among people in a religious organization are described as a "dynamic network of interconnecting elements."[3] One way of describing this is *synergy*, which is an exponential growth of the collective energy of those involved. Awareness of how this dynamic operates helps us to lead successfully by knowing the variables that exist among key stakeholders and how this affects various programs.

In an ideal situation, stakeholders set aside self-interest and come together in a reciprocally responsive relationship focused on a common purpose.[4] Most of us want to believe that the common purpose is tacitly understood by all members of our religious organization; however, we cannot afford to be that naïve. Religious leaders who lack organizational awareness tend to believe they only need to interact and communicate with one person or with a central group, such as their immediate supervisor or governing board. This approach is problematic because a religious organization is a complicated system of individuals, each with their own agendas and influence within the group. One case study comes to mind:

> James, an associate pastor, had an idea to begin an additional worship service on a new night of the week. He hoped to oversee the new service since it was his "baby." James met with the lead pastor, Sara, and delivered a passionate pitch about why the new service would be successful. Sara asked James if he had considered how starting a service on a new night might affect the various small groups already meeting in the evenings. She pointed out that the small-group leaders might get upset if attendance were adversely affected because of the new service. Sara also explained to James that holding another worship service would require the worship team to practice and perform twice as often. Sara coached James to contemplate how starting a new worship service might stretch the resources of the congregation too thin. She also advised James to think about the efficacy of the small-groups program and how important it is that this program is not abandoned. James left the meeting frustrated because Sara didn't seem to understand how impactful the new worship service could be.

In this scenario, James doesn't realize that his religious leadership exists within a larger organizational system. His idea, if carried out, would have unintended consequences for the congregation. When we learn to understand our organization as a system, we can learn how best to implement ideas and thrive as a leader. Had James considered a systemic view of his idea, he might have been able to adapt the idea to fit into the system. He also might have anticipated Sara's concerns and provided her with creative solutions. Awareness of our organizational system helps us to be better collaborators and leaders because we learn how people and programs are connected and affect one another.

Systems tend to resist change. In part, this resistance comes because those who have control of the system are unlikely to allow a change to occur unless the cost and benefits of the change are clear and justifiable. Religious organizations tend toward homeostasis, which is a term that describes how organizations and organisms seek stability and equilibrium. Like other organizations, religious organizations tend to "prefer safety over risk, survival over mission, stability over change."[5] If we engage in the kind of deep listening discussed in chapter 5, we will begin to understand that many members of a religious organization believe that preserving the status quo will give them safety from the dangers and snares of everyday life. As a result, we can face congregational norms that hold the system captive and hinder our leadership. By grasping the system, we learn how to lead our religious organization strategically despite reluctance from key stakeholders. We acquire the skill to overcome the dreaded objection: "we've always done it this way."

SURVEYING THE POLITICAL LANDSCAPE

It's helpful to think of organizational awareness as a political skill. Every organization has a political landscape that can be surveyed, and this process often has practical application for leadership. We may think of politics as a dirty business, but it is possible to enhance our political acumen while maintaining our integrity, respectfulness, and authenticity with congregants and coworkers. As Jesus taught the disciples, we should be "wise as serpents and innocent as doves" (Matthew 10:16, NRSV). Organizational awareness allows us to navigate the political landscape of our work without succumbing to deceit, obstinacy, or passive-aggressive behavior to further our agenda.

We first become skilled in the politics of our organization by understanding how resources are allocated. The concept of politics was defined by Harold Lasswell as the business of "who gets what, when, and how."[6] In other words, politics are how we obtain or retain resources for our initiatives and ongoing programs. Examples of resources in a religious organization include funding, credit for organizational successes, building space, transportation, popularity, distribution of volunteer talent, or backing from leadership. Lobbying for resources often creates conflict. Therefore, one of the chief political challenges for religious leadership is how to advocate for the resources we need without fighting over everything. In chapters 2 and 3, we wrote that emotional self-awareness and managing our ego can be helpful in these situations as we learn to choose our battles carefully.

We can also become accomplished in organizational awareness by learning how to interpret and influence policy. Every organization has a system of written and unwritten policies. Learning these policies, and the history of how they each came to exist, is crucial for us to operate effectively within our organization. Remember: it is helpful to maintain a humble attitude before we begin to challenge or change a policy, because there may have been a good reason for the policy at the time it was implemented. Maintaining a diplomatic approach regarding current policies and informal ways of operating can also help us so that we don't accidentally offend those people who were involved in drafting them in the first place. It takes deep listening and focused observation to master the way our organization works. This practice is essential if we hope to implement our leadership goals.

UNDERSTANDING AGENDAS

Everyone who operates within an organization has an agenda, which is a personal intention for gaining a particular outcome. To complicate matters, individuals may or may not be consciously aware of their own agendas. Most individual agendas are a combination of benign and noble motives, although at times they might not be constructive. To operate effectively in religious leadership, we must remember that we are working with people who have motives that may or may not align with our agenda or the stated agenda of the congregation. Knowing what motivates each person is useful to religious leaders because this is what helps us anticipate their actions.

As discussed in chapter 3, we can better understand what typically motivates each person by becoming proficient in temperament theory. For example, some people are motivated to hear public praise for their accomplishments, while others need to feel useful without drawing attention to themselves. Another model for comprehending motivation comes from William Glasser, who theorized that we are motivated by five core human needs: survival, love and belonging, power, freedom, and fun.[7] Glasser stated that each person is driven more strongly by one or more of these needs. By gaining insight into what motivates the key stakeholders in our organization, we can make educated guesses about the direction our organization might take. This intuition helps us anticipate political movement before it happens. It can also be useful as a proactive resource for exerting influence, which we address in the next chapter.

People expend energy toward their agendas, whether or not they realize they are doing so. Religious leaders need to maintain awareness of this because the energy spent by key stakeholders is what makes things happen within our congregations. Once you, as a religious leader, have carefully decided upon a course of action (e.g., a project or initiative) for your organization, one of your goals should be to gain alignment among key stakeholders before moving forward. Think about two people trying to pull the same object in different directions. Without agenda alignment, the project will not move forward with optimal speed or success because those with differing agendas will overtly or covertly work against the project. In contrast, if the project is part of a group decision among all key stakeholders, agenda alignment occurs naturally, and progress comes much easier because everyone's energy is also aligned.

Ideally, we should create as many allies as we can through honest and respectful communication. People are more likely to align with us if we listen to what is central to them, and understand why they currently hold the agenda they do. People will also respond more positively if they feel they have been treated respectfully. Maintaining their trust will have a positive impact whenever we attempt to align with them.

IMPLEMENTING IDEAS WITH ORGANIZATIONAL AWARENESS

An integral element of successful religious leadership is the implementation of our ideas and goals in the form of new initiatives. Organizational awareness can help us to launch these projects smoothly. Based on the concepts addressed previously in this chapter, the following are some practical steps to follow when we put our ideas into action:

1. Carefully analyze the reasons the project may or may not be worthwhile.
2. Double-check your motives to make sure this initiative will benefit the organization rather than meet your personal needs for community, recognition, and so on.
3. Determine the time, money, and energy needed to accomplish the project. Create a reasonable plan to obtain these resources.

Ask yourself whether the benefits of this program are worth the cost to you and the organization.

4. Identify how this project is consistent with current policy or congregational norms. If it differs with policy or norms, this challenge must be overcome first, or the project will not proceed successfully.
5. Consider how this project fits within the overall organizational system. Does it fill a legitimate need without hindering another program within the organization?
6. Build partnerships with key stakeholders by identifying their agendas and by finding practical and reasonable ways to compromise with all parties regarding the details of the project. Whenever possible, create a series of win-win-win situations so that no key stakeholder feels marginalized.
7. With the input of key stakeholders, create a tentative plan to launch the project.
8. Communicate the plan to all remaining stakeholders in concentric circles (we address this technique more fully in the next chapter).
9. Address any remaining objections and adjust the plan, within reason.
10. Launch the project and objectively evaluate ongoing input from the congregation.

ADDRESS CHALLENGES AND MINIMIZE CONFLICT

As outlined above, organizational awareness can be a useful resource when launching new projects and initiatives. Additionally, organizational awareness can help us anticipate, identify, and address ongoing threats to programs and our religious leadership. At times, we need organizational awareness to be proactive and move forward with our goals; other times, we need to be reactive as we defend ourselves from challenges to our leadership. When we are organizationally aware, we are not taken aback when these challenges occur, nor surprised by the people from whom they originate.

We can categorize people within our organization into three categories: allies, associates, and adversaries. Allies are typically willing to stand beside us and defend us amid conflict. Associates are neutral; they might not help us, but neither do they try to hurt us nor hinder our goals. Adversaries will expend energy to oppose our agenda, and sometimes they work toward hampering our overall leadership. The best strategy we can employ is to develop as many allies as possible and limit adversaries to as small a number as possible. We can also learn to accept that not every person will be our ally. Rather, we can accept them as associates without interacting with them in a way that pushes them to become an adversary.

We can avoid most conflicts by treating those we serve with courtesy and respect. By asking questions and listening to other people's ideas and concerns, we can head off most threats before they begin. With organizational awareness, we learn how to hear people, and anticipate how best to interact with each person. For example, we consider how their egos may be affected by our attitude and actions, what their agenda and motivations are, and how we can assist them with their goals. Unfortunately, not all conflict can be avoided despite our best efforts. We address how to manage these conflicts in chapter 8.

CONCLUSION

When we develop the trait of Organizational Awareness, we begin to understand group dynamics. These dynamics present challenges and opportunities for our religious leadership. We must remember that our organization is a system occupied by key stakeholders, each with motives and agendas that are highly important to them. We need to become skilled at advocating for resources and implementing programs without creating needless political adversaries. Finally, we should also be reminded that our work is not meant to fulfill all our personal needs for community or family, and this knowledge can assist us to maintain objectivity regarding our role within the organization.

In the following chapter, we explore how to utilize our organizational awareness and develop an Influential style of leadership. We look forward to taking this next step with you as you begin to put your EQ skills into action.

7

ESTABLISHING INFLUENCE

The real beginning of influence comes as others sense you are being influenced by them—when they feel understood by you—that you have listened deeply and sincerely, and that you are open.

—Stephen R. Covey[1]

We've just addressed how to become fully aware of organizational dynamics and how to operate within them. However, religious leadership requires more than simply existing in a passive state of awareness; it also requires that we know when to assert our leadership and how to influence others. There are also times when we need to be in motion and to lead people in the right direction. Leadership is knowing where you are going, and convincing others to follow.

It can be challenging to lead others without alienating them. Fortunately, strengthening our EQ trait of Influence can make it easier to lead others while keeping their trust. In this chapter, we help you develop an understanding of influence and how it is linked to our leadership. We also discuss how influence builds upon the EQ traits we've already shared with you, and how your understanding of these traits can help you put your leadership into action.

WHAT IS INFLUENCE?

The trait of Influence is defined as: "wielding a range of tactics for persuasion."[2] As religious leaders, we are influential whenever we have a positive impact on someone's faith and persuade them to make healthy life choices. This phenomenon can happen in many ways and within a variety of settings. For example, we can be highly influential and visible with large crowds of people through preaching or public speaking. In other instances, our influence can be asserted in one-on-one meetings, counseling, or in small groups. Perhaps most importantly, we can influence others by the way we treat them and the way we live our lives. Asserting our influence is often more subtle than we realize.

A major way that we can be influential is by setting a good example. The saying "practice what you preach" applies quite literally to religious leaders. Sometimes we think of this principle as only pertaining to our moral behavior, and it is true that morality is important to religious leadership. However, influencing others through example also means that we should demonstrate character traits such as kindness and humility. As one religious leader said: "The best thing is to mean what you say, and say what you mean. If people see you following up, and that you care about them, and see you celebrating their successes, they will want to follow you."[3] Another religious leader explained the need to set an example of genuineness: "People see the combination of me living the life, and preaching it, and the integrity between the two."

Several of the religious leaders we interviewed said that authenticity is integral to influence. One religious leader explained, "I guess for me one of the biggest ways I've been successful in influencing others is just by being real with people." Another church leader described how they strive for authenticity: "You can see the 'real me' if you want to; you don't have to work through a lot of levels." One pastor linked authenticity to integrity: "If you're honest with people and up front—that's how I get people to follow." In an interview with another pastor, we learned how they used authenticity to build trust and influence with their congregants: "It's just being real with people and having them understand that I'm just a real guy. I'm nobody special and no better than anyone else. I have no special powers that they don't have. I'm just here trying to help them out through this life."

Another way that religious leaders can be influential is by casting a compelling vision for their organization. Casting a vision is a vital part of leadership and one of the best ways to communicate the direction that the organization is ideally headed. As one religious leader said, "You've got to give them a vision, a direction, something worth following."

Overall, our efforts to be influential in our leadership will be enhanced if we incorporate emotion into our communication. We can learn when to be serious and straightforward, when to smile and laugh, and when to show pain and sorrow. We can also learn how to express our emotions in various settings, whether we are addressing one person, a small group, or a large crowd. One pastor explained that his influence became much stronger when he learned how to communicate with his congregation "clearly, compellingly, and from the heart."

ASSERTING OUR INFLUENCE

As religious leaders, we must learn how to assert our influence if we want to lead effectively. Assertiveness is the ability of a person to effectively and constructively communicate emotions, beliefs, and ideas.[4] In this context, asserting our influence is how we as religious leaders can honestly verbalize our feelings to our coworkers and those we serve in the most productive way possible. For example, we can assert our influence by modeling both passion and authenticity. This approach often leads to a dynamic experience in which we connect with others in ways we never have before. When we share from our heart, we can reach people in powerful ways that a logical and passionless conversation alone could never accomplish.

Your previous work with emotional self-awareness is foundational to asserting influence. Without emotional self-awareness, people remain unclear about what they really want—and are thus unable to tell others what they are feeling. It is impossible to assert how we feel about anything if we don't understand ourselves. Processing our feelings about certain people and specific circumstances gives us the chance to express ourselves with emotional clarity. It takes time and effort to sort our emotions into specific feelings that we can recognize and classify; however, using the resources provided in chapter 3 can help considerably.

When we have negative feelings about someone, we can assert that our feelings are valid and that it is healthy for us to convey our emotions to that person. This allows us to speak truthfully to that person about what we are feeling without violating his or her dignity. Then we can effectively articulate where we stand without demanding that the other person agrees with us. This clears the air without provoking the other person into an argument, and it invites the person to be candid with us as well. Consider the following example that was reported to us of how to address a misunderstanding between two religious leaders:

> Michelle was an associate pastor who worked with another associate pastor named Dan. In one instance, Dan made a comment in a staff meeting about Michelle that she felt made her look incompetent in front of her coworkers and boss. Michelle was resentful of this for three days, and she noticed that her relationship with Dan had become strained during this time. She finally decided to discuss her feelings with Dan and she scheduled a meeting with him to do so. Michelle thanked Dan for giving her time to meet, then shared how she felt about his comment at the prior meeting. Dan was very surprised to learn that Michelle felt this way, and he immediately apologized and reassured Michelle that he meant no harm. Michelle was gracious and accepted Dan's apology. Both Dan and Michelle were thankful for the chance to communicate with one another, and their professional relationship and mutual respect improved dramatically because of the meeting.

There are three basic types of conversation or personal interaction that can occur between two people: passive, aggressive, and assertive. When religious leaders are passive, we surrender our ability to share feelings by permitting the other person to be in control of the conversation. Conversely, if we use an aggressive approach, we will take charge of the conversation and deny the other party's opportunity for expression. In contrast, asserting our influence is neither passive nor aggressive. Rather, it is a two-way interaction based on mutual respect. This is a sweet middle ground where we can present our feelings without invalidating the feelings of anyone else. To paraphrase Lou Gerstner: "It's about emotional honesty. . . . You communicate, and you communicate, and you communicate."[5]

We can also be assertive to communicate positive emotions. For example, when we tell people that we appreciate them, we are asserting how we feel about them. It can be easy to spend our time and energy only on the negative aspects of religious leadership, such as times when people disappoint us or aggravate us. However, if we can share affirming feedback with others more often than negative comments, they are more likely to respond favorably. As Donald Miller wrote: "Nobody will listen to you unless they sense that you like them."[6]

We can further reinforce good behavior by encouraging our coworkers and congregants whenever they do something right.[7] We create a "self-fulfilling prophecy" of positive behavior when we communicate that we think highly of others, even before they have proven themselves. Typically, people will want to do their best to match the expectation we set, whether it be positive or negative. If we show that our opinion of them is high, people will often strive not to let us down. This powerful interaction can lead to a healthy and productive relationship based on mutual trust and respect. This will allow us to influence those we serve to become the best possible people they can be: "Therefore, encourage one another and build each other up" (I Thess. 5:11).[8]

It is also important for us to give credit to people who contribute toward a project or program at every stage of the work. We can do this publicly or privately, depending upon what we believe is appropriate at a given point in time. This is likely to encourage them to see the project through and to contribute the next time their help is requested. Remember, giving encouragement costs us nothing, so there is no point in holding back genuine praise. As a general principle, people want to feel as if they have contributed to something worthwhile, and the work that individuals perform within religious organizations is no different. As one pastor stated: "People want to be part of something bigger than themselves." Therefore, when we show our appreciation for people and what they do, we assert our influence and make a tremendous impact on individual people and the whole organization.

Warning: religious leaders are highly influential because of the position and title they hold. The power differential between us and those we serve must not be misused. If we assert our influence to mislead anyone to promote our personal agenda, we violate the bonds of a sacred trust. It is imperative to remember that our primary mission is always to promote the faith and well-being of those in our care, and to lead with impeccable integrity.

ASSERTING INFLUENCE FOR
TRANSFORMATIONAL LEADERSHIP

One of the practical ways we can assert our influence is with a transformational style of leadership. Transformational leadership is defined as a leadership style that "inspires people to achieve unexpected or remarkable results."[9] With transformational leadership, we can communicate to individuals that we care about and believe in them. Then we can show them how to develop their potential and feel like a valuable part of the organization. To accomplish this, we must first learn to understand people and see their best qualities. This is done through our knowledge of temperament theory, as discussed in chapter 3. We can also show them empathy, as discussed extensively in chapter 5. As we deepen our understanding of people, we can recognize their gifts and what motivates them to serve.

As our relationship with people deepens, we can discover ways for them to grow within the context of our religious organization. With a little determination and creativity, we can typically find an opportunity for every person to feel useful according to their giftedness. This plan may look different for each person, especially within the roles of volunteers and staff. With emotional intelligence, we can learn how to guide each person toward personal growth in an empathetic manner that accurately accounts for individuality. We can also learn how to collaborate with people, so they can be partners in their own development.

Unfortunately, as religious leaders we can sometimes be guilty of placing people in roles for which they are not well suited. This error can happen when we don't fully understand a person, or because we had a role that needed to be filled with some urgency. When this occurs, we create a lose-lose situation for the organization and for that individual. We can avoid this blunder by considering each person as uniquely capable, and accepting our responsibility as religious leaders to influence people in ways that align with their temperaments. For example, are we placing introverted people in crowd-facing roles, and extroverts in quiet, isolated positions? Each of these temperament types should not be placed in situations that fail to promote their success.

In the book *The Tao of Pooh*, Benjamin Hoff used an ancient Chinese teaching from Chuang-tse to explain this principle:

Hui-tse said to Chuang-tse, "I have a large tree which no carpenter can cut into lumber. Its branches and trunk are crooked and tough, covered with bumps and depressions. No builder would turn his head to look at it. Your teachings are the same—useless, without value. Therefore, no one pays attention to them."

"As you know," Chuang-tse replied, "a cat is very skilled at capturing its prey. Crouching low, it can leap in any direction, pursuing whatever it is after. But when its attention is focused on such things, it can be easily caught with a net. On the other hand, a huge yak it not easily caught or overcome. It stands like a stone, or a cloud in the sky. But for all its strength, it cannot catch a mouse.

"You complain that your tree is not valuable as lumber. But you could make use of the shade it provides, rest under its sheltering branches, admiring its sheltering branches, and stroll beneath it, admiring its character and appearance. Since it would not be endangered by an ax, what could threaten its existence? It is useless to you only because you want to make it into something else and do not use it in its proper way."[10]

From this passage, we learn that everyone can be valuable to our organization once their gifts are recognized. We can deftly assert our influence by finding opportunities that fit each person. We can also teach people to trust in themselves by demonstrating how highly we think of them and their enormous potential. Once people believe that they can be useful and successful, they will transform into stronger and healthier individuals. They will also persevere with their responsibilities longer and enjoy more personal fulfillment because their gifts are correctly aligned with their duties. Finally, people can learn to appreciate the contributions of others because they feel more self-confident. Therefore, we can use transformational leadership to encourage individuals to believe in themselves, to respect those around them, and to fulfill their immense promise.

INFLUENCE THROUGH COMMUNICATION TECHNIQUES

Another practical way that we can assert our influence is with strategic communication techniques. Many religious leaders discover that the efficacy of their leadership is strongly affected by the way they communicate with the key stakeholders in the organization, as discussed in chapter 6. This is especially true when it comes to installing new programs, initiatives, or policy changes. Purposefully planning a communication strategy can save us a lot of trouble and aid our initiative or new program to launch successfully. Asserting our influence can assist the communication process considerably because it provides clarity and purpose to our message.

When launching a new program, it is important to identify the key stakeholders and how much influence each of them might have in the success (or sabotage) of our initiative. This can look a little different for each religious leader, depending on the makeup of our organizational structure and the role we play within it. It helps to visualize this concept as moving outward through concentric circles.

Imagine a target where we begin in the center with the people who have the most influence and investment. Moving outward, each of the larger circles would contain a set of people with varying levels of influence. Our goal is to work our way through each circle of people until we reach the outer edge of the target. By communicating strategically with people at each level, we can secure precious buy-in from key stakeholders. This allows us to gain political momentum and allies along the way. This process is called consensus building, and it is a very potent method that helps us to assert our influence and demonstrate our leadership.[11] One pastor explained how he purposefully used consensus building to gain support for a new program: "At the end of the day, there were multiple layers of approvals that I needed. I needed approval from my senior pastor, board of elders, and district. I had to work with over 100 plus people to join with us in starting it, spouse, kids, good friends, and all of that."[12]

A word of advice: When devising your communication strategy, never try to go around the organizational chain of command to get an initiative approved. This will only create an unpleasant conflict and erode trust with your immediate supervisor(s) because you went "behind their back." Consensus building is not meant to be secretive or manipulative. It is simply a practical method for us to assert our influence and communicate effectively within the structure of our organization. As with all opportunities for communication, our ideas will be received better if we address everyone involved with honesty and respect.

CONCLUSION

Learning how to assert our influence is a necessary transition for us to undergo as religious leaders. If we fail to assert our influence, we will be passive leaders who lack the ability to guide others. Conversely, if we are too aggressive, we will alienate the people around us and lose the chance to make a positive impact in their lives.

Even after learning how to assert our influence, along with the understanding gained regarding the trait of Organizational Awareness in chapter 6, we can still find ourselves amid difficult conflict. In the next chapter, we address how to manage conflicts effectively. We also discuss how to view these situations as valuable opportunities to elevate our religious leadership.

8

EMBRACING CONFLICT MANAGEMENT

The goal of resolving conflict in a relationship is not victory or defeat.
It's reaching understanding and letting go of our need to be right.
—Catrienne McGuire[1]

Among all the EQ traits we've covered, our research and experience have shown that Conflict Management is the skill that religious leaders need most urgently. This is because most of our work happens with people, and conflict among human beings is inevitable when given enough time and exposure to one another. In some cases, we can prevent conflict from occurring by exercising the EQ traits learned in this book. For example, we can utilize Emotional Self-Control to keep from losing our temper, Empathy to prevent ourselves from alienating others, and Organizational Awareness to anticipate political challenges. However, we (the authors) have learned through our varied experiences that conflict can still erupt within religious organizations, despite our best efforts. With the trait of Conflict Management, religious leaders can keep many of these disputes from becoming worse, and in many cases, disarm the conflict entirely.

Many of the religious leaders we interviewed expressed that conflict management is the hardest EQ trait to master. Most of them explained that they received very little training in managing conflict as part of their formal education. To add to the problem, many of us have a strong need to be liked by others, and this inhibits our motivation to address conflict. Many religious leaders mistakenly assume that they won't have to struggle with conflict because religious organizations are "big, happy families," as discussed in chapter 6. Fortunately, we can develop the trait of Conflict Management so that working with conflict doesn't have to be nearly as intimidating or difficult.

WHAT IS CONFLICT MANAGEMENT?

Conflict happens when two parties disagree with one another, and when being right is more important to them than anything else. In religious organizations, conflict can be a disagreement about how people think congregational resources should be allocated, a potential change in organizational policy or norms, or a clash of personalities that escalates to unfortunate levels. In some cases, the conflict arises among our coworkers or our congregants, and we are left with the difficult task of mediating between the contestants. Other times, the conflict involves us directly, and we face the challenge of defusing frustration that others feel toward us.

Religious leaders in noncongregational settings also experience conflict. Hospital chaplains, for example, report they experience conflict relative to theological differences with hospital staff or other chaplains. Also, school administrators and teachers who work in religious settings experience conflict between the expectations of parents and students, and what their institution can actually deliver within budgetary, policy, and time constraints. Military and prison chaplains also experience conflict, especially with regulations and institutional hierarchy. Additionally, conflict relative to the allocation of scarce resources is common in all these settings.

Conflict Management is a trait that allows us to listen and understand the perspective of all parties in the disagreement. It also helps us to lead everyone toward a fair compromise. Furthermore, it helps us to identify and respectfully address the conflict with each person, so they do not become resentful or passive-aggressive. Finally, conflict management helps us to adopt a more positive perspective of conflict in general. When conflict arises, we can view it as an opportunity to repair relationships, to help people heal and grow, and to demonstrate our leadership by facilitating a peaceful and productive resolution.

CONFLICT CAN BE DESTRUCTIVE TO OTHERS

Without EQ, the way we address conflict can be incredibly destructive to those we serve. One of the first principles we must remember when conflict arises is the need to consistently "speak the truth in love" (Ephesians 4:15a, ESV). Otherwise, we will emotionally wound the people who disagree with us, especially if we fail to speak with humility and gentleness. Also, we can minimize conflict if we respond to people with an attitude of kindness when they are upset or angry. As the proverb teaches, "A gentle answer turns away wrath" (Proverbs 15:1). Remember, we are in religious leadership to build up those we serve, not to tear them down with harsh or careless language.

It is very important to remember that we must never invoke divine principles just to win a dispute. This behavior becomes especially destructive if we imply that a person has disappointed God, or if we suggest that they are "out of God's will." We must never manipulate those we serve with language that evokes shame. This is an egregious misuse of power, and the psychological damage caused by this communication style can be long-lasting. As Maya Angelou wrote: "I've learned that people will forget what you said, people will forget what you did, but people will never forget how you made them feel."[2] Remember, our position of leadership with the people we serve is one of sacred trust, and we should take this honor very seriously.

Fortunately, the trait of Conflict Management can be combined with other EQ traits to limit the damage done to others in the throes of conflict. For instance, we can call upon the trait of Emotional Self-Awareness to question our own motives and level of emotional investment during a conflict. We might ask ourselves, "How are my previous experiences or traumas contributing to my part in this dispute?" For example, we might realize that we have difficulty backing down from disagreements because we dislike feeling powerless. When we do this, we can acknowledge our discomfort, move ahead with compassion for ourselves and others, and learn that we can survive the feeling of powerlessness within the situation. Later, we can use what we learn from the experience in our ongoing process of deepening self-awareness toward becoming more emotionally and spiritually mature. This can ultimately make us more effective when we face conflict again.

The trait of Empathy can also be helpful in dealing with conflict because it allows us to understand the perspective of those embroiled within it. We can anticipate how each person might be feeling and why they might be feeling that way. Furthermore, we can use the trait of Emotional Self-Control to recognize and manage our feelings to find productive solutions. Otherwise, we might allow our negative feelings to come barreling forth during the heat of an argument and say things we will regret.

CONFLICT CAN BE DESTRUCTIVE TO OUR ORGANIZATION

Unresolved conflict can be destructive to organizations, so it is imperative that we address it as religious leaders. For example, a conflict that is improperly handled can lead to the rancorous departure of a member from our organization. On a larger scale, an organizational split can occur when a conflict is not successfully dealt with, and one person (or family) decides to leave the organization and take others along with them. Regrettably, some people will leave our organization, even when we've done everything we can to resolve their concerns. The following story illustrates how difficult it can be to prevent congregants from leaving:

> Once upon a time, a man was shipwrecked on a deserted island. He was an industrious, hard-working sort of man, so by the time he was rescued, fifteen years later, he had managed to transform the island into a collection of roads and buildings. The people who rescued him were amazed at his accomplishments and asked for a tour of the island. He was more than happy to oblige.
>
> "The first building on our left," he began, "is my house. You'll see that I have a comfortable three-bedroom estate, complete with indoor plumbing and a sprinkler system. There is also a storage shed in the back for all my lawn tools." The rescue party was astonished. It was better than some of their homes on the mainland.
>
> "That building over there is the store where I do my grocery shopping. Next to it is my bank, and across the street is the gym where I exercise."

The rescuers noticed two other buildings and asked what they were. "The one on the left is where I go to church."

"And the one on the right?" they inquired.

"Oh, that's where I *used* to go to church."[3]

It's quite challenging to rectify every grievance that congregants have against our religious organization and with us. However, with EQ, we can reduce the number of people who leave because of poorly handled conflict.

CONFLICT CAN BE DESTRUCTIVE TO US

As religious leaders, we tend to put our own needs last, as discussed in chapter 2. However, we can learn how to manage conflicts so that we are not hurt unnecessarily. One of the main ways we can do this is by establishing healthy boundaries for ourselves. For instance, we can become resolute about the way we allow others to speak to us, our families, and our staff. We should expect to be treated with respect and common courtesy. We establish this standard for ourselves by communicating it to others. The alternative is for us to allow ourselves to become emotionally damaged by people whenever they feel like abusing us, and this habit does not honor God's intentions for us. Aren't we just as important to God as the people we serve?

We can also learn to protect ourselves when conflict arises by practicing careful documentation. This is a practice that requires discipline, but it is worth the extra effort. Every time we have a meeting or conversation that involves conflict, we need to take careful notes that include the date and time of the conversation, the nature of the conflict, who was involved, what was said, and how we managed the problem. Sending an email message to all participants in the conflict that includes any decisions made can help clarify the outcomes for everyone. It can also serve as a reminder to those who may not remember the situation in the same way. Documentation can also be accomplished by archiving our email correspondence for future reference. We should also alert our immediate supervisor or governing board of potential and ongoing conflicts as quickly as possible.

When reporting conflicts to our superiors, it is important to exercise emotional self-control and maintain a professional demeanor. In so doing, we should report the content of the conflict and who was involved without offering personal opinions. As religious leaders, we must set a high standard for how to deal with and communicate about conflict. Reporting only factual information should be the norm, rather than including disparaging or demeaning comments about any individuals or groups. Supervisors and governing boards have a responsibility to avoid sharing this information with others who are not involved, just as we have a responsibility to refrain from involving others inappropriately. It is also important to provide updates to our superiors at appropriate intervals, and to make recommendations about next steps. This overall approach allows us to act professionally, maintain credibility, and demonstrate that we can keep a level head when facing difficult circumstances.

OUR INTERNAL CONFLICTS

Many of the difficult interpersonal challenges we experience as religious leaders originate from our own internal conflicts. For example, our ego can become inflamed during an argument. There are times in our lives when our ego emerges as a tyrant that must be satisfied, as discussed in chapter 2. This can happen especially when we are vulnerable, such as times of illness, when we are experiencing problems within our own families, or during times of difficult transitions. Examples of challenging life transitions include moving to a new setting, undergoing big changes within our support system, experiencing a shift in our ideologies and sense of purpose, facing retirement, and considering our own mortality.

In situations where we are more susceptible to the dictates of our ego, winning the argument can feel more important to us than preserving the relationship. This can lead to an unfortunate escalation of the conflict and the needless loss of a congregant, staff member, colleague, or friend. In contrast, when we remain emotionally self-aware amid conflict, we can examine our attitude and responses while maintaining a kind and humble attitude.

Without EQ, our internal doubts and fears can cause unhealthy and unmanageable levels of internal conflict. For instance, we can assume the worst about people's motives when they disagree with us. When we give license to these anxieties, we may begin to believe that people are conspiring to bring about our downfall. This can lead to strained relationships and fractured trust. Therefore, assuming the worst motives of people can lead to an unfortunate self-fulfilling prophecy.

We must never allow our suspicious tendencies to rule our thoughts or dominate our hearts. This also applies to the personal insecurities we sometimes entertain, which can badly cloud our judgment regarding how others think of us. The reality is that most people don't think about us nearly as much as we think they do. Unfortunately, the trust that people place in our leadership can become eroded when we project an insecure and needy persona. Ultimately, we can help ourselves tremendously by not worrying about whether or not others like us. Remember: "what other people think about you is none of your business."[4]

Another way we can intensify conflict is if we allow ourselves to become bitter, which is easy to do when we feel hurt or betrayed. To illustrate this point, imagine that each of us has an internal, balancing scale that represents our individual sense of justice. When people hurt us, our personal scale gets knocked out of balance. As a result, we attempt to balance the scale and mete out justice by locking that person "in jail" in our heart. This phenomenon is commonly known as holding a resentment or grudge, and this is an extremely unhealthy practice. As the saying goes, "resentment is like taking poison and waiting for the other person to die."[5] Unfortunately, we will never heal while we hold a grudge, and the relationship with that person won't improve either. If we don't forgive, we will always have conflict with that person because our heart will project it unconsciously. As Donald Miller wrote:

> When I am talking to someone, there are always two conversations going on. The first is on the surface; it is about politics or music or whatever it is that our mouths are saying. The other is beneath the surface, on the level of the heart, and my heart is either communicating that I like the person I am talking to or I don't. God wants both conversations to be true.[6]

Remember, God expects us to forgive our judgments against others, and not just when they apologize: "Be kind and compassionate to one another, forgiving each other, just as in Christ, God forgave you" (Ephesians 4:32, NIV).

MANAGING CONFLICT IS NECESSARY

Because conflict can be destructive, we must manage it properly. First, we must realize that conflicts often worsen unless the problem is handled effectively. As one religious leader said: "I address things. I don't let things lie. Some people turn their head and hope it goes away, and it never will. You have to address things."[7] Another religious leader explained how he faces disagreements head-on, listens to the perspective of all parties, and redirects the negative energy of conflict toward a useful purpose:

> It's not being afraid of conflicts and healthy tension. It's directing it in a way that's actually helpful. It's more like, help me to understand why you are feeling what you are feeling, and thinking the way you're thinking, and in responding the way you're responding, because I think you're seeing something that I'm not seeing. So help me understand.[8]

Religious leaders have a particularly important role within conflict. As religious and spiritual leaders, we are teachers and guides. Whether we are leaders of religious organizations, chaplains, spiritual directors, counselors, or leaders of social action agencies, our charge is the same: to be agents of healing, peace, love, grace, compassion, and hope. We cannot fully answer our call if we do not learn how to manage conflict in healthy and productive ways.

CONFLICT CREATES OPPORTUNITIES

When conflict occurs, we are afforded an important opportunity to clear the air among all parties, including times when the dispute involves us. When this process is successful, it can lead to healing of relationships because everyone has been able to communicate and to feel heard. Then, trust can be built because all individuals have been honest while still feeling respected. Ultimately, we can learn how to disagree with one another without our differences leading to resentment. In fact, well-managed conflicts can strengthen relationships. For example, one religious leader described how she learned to fight fairly with her coworker: "I like to say that we fought well. We actually enjoyed it. We would go at it, and then afterward, one of us would poke our head in the other's office, and ask: 'We good?' The other one of us would reply, 'Yep, we're good.'"

Conflict can also provide an opportunity for us to help *others* grow. Consider the example provided by Jesus and his leadership. He was an encouraging leader, but he also admonished people when needed. Jesus did not attempt to preserve harmony at all costs; he understood that confrontation is unavoidable if we want to help people become healthier and stronger individuals. As religious leaders, it is important that we learn from Jesus's example and not be afraid to "call out" unhealthy attitudes or behaviors as the situation requires. To properly lead, we must know when boldness and confrontation are the best way to reach people and ignite their personal growth. As the humorist Finley Peter Dunne wrote in the early 1900s, we should be willing to "comfort the afflicted, and afflict the comforted."[9]

Conflict also creates an opportunity for *our organizations* to grow. As religious leaders, we should utilize all the resources available to us, including various ideas from other people. For instance, we can solicit the input of others when developing initiatives, even when their ideas disagree with ours. Conflict management allows us to synthesize different ideas into a creative plan that helps our organizations. It also helps us to be diplomatic whenever someone's opinion is not incorporated into the plan. The effective management of conflict provides opportunities for rich collaboration that our organizations would not otherwise experience.

Finally, we cannot grow as *individuals* without conflict. Conflict forces us to consider different perspectives and to push ourselves to higher levels of maturity. Consider the example of the butterfly and how it breaks free from the cocoon; it is the difficult struggle that gives strength to its wings. Similarly, people who embrace conflict become emotionally and spiritually stronger. When we manage conflict, we learn a lot about ourselves and how to handle uncomfortable and difficult interpersonal situations.

PRACTICAL SUGGESTIONS TO MANAGE CONFLICT

Conflict should be managed correctly to minimize the damage done to us, to others, and to our organizations. We can also view conflict as an opportunity to lead others toward reconciliation, healing, and growth. The following are some practical suggestions we can use to facilitate successful conflict resolution:

- When someone approaches you with a concern or offense, never minimize that person's feelings. Everyone's feelings are honest and real.
- Listen with empathy to the person's concern and make sure you understand what you are being told (see chapter 5). Make sure the person feels heard by you.
- Ask yourself if there is a simple solution to the concern. If so, offer the solution to the concerned party and ask if this plan sounds suitable.
- If the person desires a complicated solution (e.g., it involves other stakeholders, contradicts policy, disrupts current programs, is expensive), communicate the various challenges to the other person so that the cost of what the person is suggesting can be understood.
- If the person does not offer any options that might resolve his or her concern, ask the person to help find a reasonable solution. This can empower him or her to work toward a fair resolution of the problem.
- If a conflict within the organization comes to your attention indirectly, investigate the concern, evaluate the risk it poses, and create a plan to intervene as needed.
- When the conflict involves hurt feelings between two parties, attempt to get them together to clear the air. This meeting should remain respectful at all times.
- Encourage both parties to hear and understand each other's point of view, forgive each other, and find a reasonable compromise whenever possible. If the offense is with you, do your best to apologize humbly and make amends (Matthew 5:24).
- If someone has hurt *you*, ask to speak to that person privately and tell him or her how you feel. Do not involve anyone else in the

conflict until you have exhausted all efforts to reconcile directly with the person who hurt you (Matthew 18:15).

- If the conflict has spread to other people who were not part of the original offense, attempt to resolve the issue with the original parties, and then work your way outward in concentric circles as discussed in chapter 7. As one religious leader said: "You just have to win them over one at a time."
- Throughout the process, strive to keep your heart free of bitterness and attempt to maintain an attitude of compassion, patience, and kindness.
- Maintain healthy boundaries for yourself and everyone else involved in the conflict.
- Remember that not all conflicts can be resolved, even when we manage the situation diligently and conduct ourselves with humility.

CONCLUSION

Managing conflict within our religious organizations can feel like a daunting and thankless task. However, conflict can create unique opportunities for growth that we can recognize and appreciate as we develop emotional intelligence. It can also provide a platform for us to demonstrate leadership as we facilitate healing and reconciliation among those we serve. Conflict also allows us to learn more about ourselves, and how we can better interact with others. It's important to remember that unaddressed or poorly handled conflict can hurt individuals, erode relationships, and ultimately, damage organizations. With EQ, we can manage conflict with skill and confidence as it arises. As Thomas Paine wrote: "The harder the conflict, the more glorious the triumph."[10] For religious leaders, that triumph begets emotional and spiritual healing within the communities we serve and within ourselves.

9

SPIRITUALITY OF THE EMOTIONALLY INTELLIGENT RELIGIOUS LEADER

The spiritual life is not a life before, after, or beyond our everyday existence. No, the spiritual life can only be real when it is lived in the midst of the pains and joys of the here and now. Therefore, we need to begin with a careful look at the way we think, speak, feel, and act from hour to hour, day to day, week to week, and year to year, in order to become more fully aware of our hunger for [God].

—Henry Nouwen[1]

In previous chapters, we have described six traits of emotional intelligence and have guided you through an examination of your own growth as an emotionally intelligent religious leader. We have tied the traits together progressively so that you can become ever-more effective in your work. In some of the chapters, we moved beyond religious leadership and referred to spiritual leadership to prepare you for this chapter. Our emotions are connected to our spirituality, and so it would be inappropriate for us to ignore your spiritual self as we guide you in your overall development.

Even though this book focuses on emotional intelligence, our development as human beings doesn't happen only within our emotions. As humans, we are physical, intellectual, emotional, *and* spiritual beings. "Spirituality is a way of life that affects and includes every moment of existence. It is at once a contemplative attitude, a disposition to a life of depth, and the search for ultimate meaning, direction, and belonging."[2] As religious leaders, we have a responsibility to live out our spirituality through the ways in which we communicate and behave. With focus and practice, we can do so in an emotionally intelligent manner.

EMOTIONAL INTELLIGENCE AND SPIRITUALITY

Each of the EQ traits we've covered in this book has a spiritual application. For example, as we deepen our Emotional Self-Awareness (chapters 2 and 3), we release ourselves from the bondage of needing to maintain the façade of our "false self." In so doing, we become more accepting of ourselves with our human imperfections. We also begin to deeply accept the love and grace that God freely offers to us, and replace our feelings of condemnation and shame with compassion toward ourselves. Once this happens, our relationship with God can flourish.

As we become more emotionally self-aware, we also become more cognizant of the times when we act emotionally and overreact to situations. Our spirituality is not just about our relationship with God; it is also dependent on how we treat others. God expects us to love one another; this is part of our spiritual covenant; for "those who do not love a brother or sister whom they have seen, cannot love God whom they have not seen" (1 John 4:20b, ESV). Therefore, as we strengthen our Emotional Self-Control (chapter 4), we can be less at the mercy of the intense negative emotions that are destructive to our relationships. In turn, improving our relationships frees up our energy so that we can focus more on activities and practices through which we can grow spiritually. Once again, our spiritual growth happens in an ever-deepening cycle that can positively affect every aspect of our lives.

When we understand how our emotional reactions affect others, we are better able to connect with them. Then we can understand their struggles and adopt the trait of Empathy, as discussed in chapter 5. Once this happens, we can comprehend the magnitude of God's grace and remember the multitude of ways that God loves and forgives us. As we experience this connection more acutely, we cannot avoid becoming more empathic and more naturally able to respond to others lovingly and compassionately. Once we learn to empathize with others, we can expand our perception to the broader sphere of Organizational Awareness (chapter 6). We can then realize the spiritual effect that we have within our organization, and the effect people in our organization have on us. "Indeed, the body does not consist of one member, but of many" (I Corinthians 12:14, NRSV). As Pope Francis wrote:

> Loving others is a spiritual force drawing us to union with God. . . . When we live out a spirituality of drawing nearer to others and see-ing their welfare, our hearts are opened wide to the Lord's greatest and most beautiful gifts. Whenever we encounter another person in love, we learn something new about God. Whenever our eyes are opened to acknowledge the other, we grow in the light of faith and knowledge of God. [3]

Additionally, we can assert a positive influence within our organiza-tion if we consciously and continuously live a spiritual life. If we only talk about spirituality, but no one sees any evidence of it, our leadership will be marred by our inauthenticity. How can we teach what we do not really understand and demonstrate? We cannot. As we shared about the trait of Influence in chapter 7, we can communicate our passion and our vision both verbally and nonverbally. Oftentimes, we can influence others more through our own spirituality than with our religious rheto-ric. If we are uncomfortable sharing our personal spirituality with oth-ers, a good way to move forward might be to share our discomfort and invite them to join us in exploring spirituality together. How refreshing it might be to realize that the leader doesn't know everything!

We ended chapter 8 by referring to the spiritual healing that can take place within ourselves and others when we manage conflict in a positive way. We can learn a lot about God during times of conflict if we keep an open mind and heart. Ultimately, conflict creates an opportu-nity for our perceptions to be challenged and for God to teach us in new ways. This process can lead to a remarkable experience of spiritual healing because we are no longer mired in outgrown perspectives.

SPIRITUAL MATURITY

Much of our work as religious leaders requires us to not only have emotional maturity, but spiritual maturity, as well. Unfortunately, as discussed in other chapters, it happens all too often that we get so wrapped up in the duties of our religious leadership, and we neglect our spirituality. In so doing, we neglect our sacred connection with God and our growth ceases. If we want to continue growing, we must do so with intentionality. Otherwise, our spirituality can diminish, even while we are doing "God's work." Peter Scazzero explained this problem as "doing for God," rather than "being with God."[4]

To gain spiritual maturity, we must find a way to set aside the chaos we experience as religious leaders. To do so, we must seek solitude so we can focus on our relationship with God. It is in these quiet times that we are drawn "into the depths of our being, where we come face to face with ourselves, our weaknesses, and with the ultimate mystery [of God]."[5] Therefore, when we choose to spend time with God, we create a powerful moment in which we can grow and mature.

SPIRITUAL PRACTICE

You may wonder how you will ever get anything accomplished if you must spend so much time alone with God. We as authors understand that your role as a religious leader is full of activity and responsibility, and your schedule does not allow for large segments of uninterrupted spiritual devotion. The key is to carve out consistent time alone with God without neglecting your leadership duties. In chapter 3, we discussed several practical methods to enhance our emotional self-awareness, such as meditation, contemplative prayer, and journaling. These can also be used to develop our spirituality amid our busy lives.

The balance between listening to God and serving others is possible if we are diligent and intentional in our pursuit of a well-rounded spiritual life and practice. Spiritual practice can take many forms, and it's important that you discover methods that work with your temperament, lifestyle, and the demands of your life within your work and your family. Here are a few ideas of how to focus on your spiritual practice that you may not have considered:

- Try verbalizing a spiritual phrase, greeting, or blessing to a stranger. It's amazing how this small act can bring about a spiritual awakening. It requires that you take a risk and share your spirituality in a new way. Use a traditional phrase that you know, research a new phrase, or make up your own.

- Leave your office or place of work and take a walk, preferably outdoors. Be sure to adopt a posture that shows you are not "open for business" by lowering your eyes and focusing on your stride. Some people like to count their steps, while others prefer to focus on a particular word or phrase that provides inspiration or comfort.
- If available, walk a labyrinth. Some churches and hospitals have invested in having one created on their grounds as a space for walking in meditation. The best part of this method is that everyone knows the rules: "You don't talk when you're walking the labyrinth."
- Purchase or create a desk labyrinth. Close your office door (with a "do not disturb" sign) and give yourself at least five minutes to "walk" the labyrinth with your finger, following it with your eyes. You may want to silently repeat a word or phrase if you cannot empty your mind.
- Stop whenever you can, close your eyes momentarily, and breathe in and out very slowly for at least five breaths. Each breath in, and each breath out should be held to the count of five. As you breathe in, think: "Breathing in cleansing air; breathing out all my concerns." You can make up any other phrase that will serve you in the moment.
- Take time to practice *lectio divina*. This is a method taught in many seminaries in which you read a scriptural passage aloud, pause for silence, and read it aloud again. Notice what word or phrase catches your attention, pause again, then read it one more time. At the end of the reading, you can meditate or pray with the word or phrase foremost in your mind. This method also lends itself to being practiced in a group setting.
- Enroll in a silent retreat of at least one day, preferably in a natural setting. Some are arranged for a weekend, and others for a full week. Make sure that there are leaders who can guide and support you if the silence brings up emotional issues. This is an advanced spiritual method, so we recommend you gain some experience with prolonged silence before committing to a retreat.

With creativity and just a little research, you can find many other ways to focus on your spirituality.

CONCLUSION

We've just asked you to become conscious of your connection with God, to commit to spiritual practice, and to consider how the six EQ traits are connected to your spiritual maturity. Emotional maturity provides the ability to be resilient and adaptable as you address the challenges of your work. In contrast, spiritual maturity grounds you in the foundation of your call to serve God. Spiritual growth is a personal journey that transcends your role in religious leadership and will continue throughout your lifetime. We pray that your path leads you ever closer to God.

10

CONCLUSION

When dealing with people, remember you are not dealing with creatures of logic, but with creatures of emotion.

—Dale Carnegie[1]

Emotional intelligence has a positive effect on our individual growth, our interpersonal relationships, and the effectiveness of our religious leadership. Without it, we are left with the burden of leading others through difficult, sometimes traumatic, circumstances without our full complement of emotional and spiritual resources. Adding to our leadership challenges, we work with people in a sacred context, which amplifies the emotional and spiritual risks posed to others and ourselves. Many religious leaders have found that their training in theology alone was not enough to prepare them for the rigors of their job. This book has covered the EQ traits of Emotional Self-Awareness, Emotional Self-Control, Empathy, Organizational Awareness, Influence, and Conflict Management. More specifically, we've discussed how these traits can be developed to improve your professional resilience and personal spirituality. This can help you realize your enormous potential as religious and spiritual leaders.

The trait of Emotional Self-Awareness is foundational to the rest of EQ development. Without it, we are unable to embrace the humility needed to grow as individuals. As religious leaders, we often face struggles with our ego and perfectionism, which can be harmful if not recognized and addressed. Emotional self-awareness can help us learn our strengths and weaknesses and how to use this knowledge to bolster and improve our leadership efforts. As we develop greater self-awareness, less of our life will be lived while on "autopilot," and more of it can be experienced with an ability to make better choices for ourselves. The lifelong journey of emotional self-awareness requires tremendous courage as we confront our shadow, trusting that we will be stronger and more effective leaders as a result of this process. It's important to remember that, with greater self-awareness, we inevitably discover that many more choices are available to us than we ever imagined.

The trait of Emotional Self-Control is also important. We need to check our emotional responses and the effect we have on others before we act. At the same time, we can acknowledge that emotions are very powerful and require expression. They also must be processed in healthy ways. This balance can be especially challenging for us as religious leaders because we work with people, and our interactions with them can evoke strong feelings within us. Through the use of emotional self-control, we can also learn to protect ourselves and elevate our job satisfaction. We can do this by setting emotional boundaries, practicing consistent self-care, and recognizing our emotional triggers.

Moving beyond ourselves, we need to have the trait of Empathy for others and to refrain from judging or condemning those we encounter. The alternative is to exacerbate the deep feelings of shame that plague so many individuals. We can gain empathy for others by learning to listen deeply to them and their concerns, so they feel they have been heard. By acting out of compassion for others, we can be agents of hope and healing when they need it most. We can also be careful of pushing ourselves into compassion fatigue and remain aware that our family needs empathy from us, too.

Similarly, we must listen to others and understand their point of view. This can assist us in developing the trait of Organizational Awareness. An organization's emotional state can have a large impact on our overall leadership. It is essential to view our organization systemically, survey the political landscape, and understand the agendas of key stakeholders. By doing this, we can develop effective strategies to motivate others, address challenges, and minimize conflict. Overall, the more we understand group dynamics and how they apply to our organization, the more successful our religious leadership will be.

We must assert our influence within our organization. Setting a good example and remaining authentic are excellent first steps toward establishing trust and confidence in our leadership. We can also exert influence by sharing a compelling vision and communicating from the heart. Our influence can be asserted in both positive and negative ways. Ideally, we will utilize transformational leadership and help people achieve remarkable results for themselves and our organizations. We can also maximize our leadership opportunities by communicating effectively and strategically. Overall, we can remember that Influence is one of the key traits that define leadership.

Perhaps most importantly, it is imperative that we utilize the trait of Conflict Management. If ignored or mishandled, conflict can be quite destructive to others, our organizations, and to us. Additionally, if we do not address our internal struggles, they can intensify our interpersonal conflicts. However, conflict can present surprising opportunities for growth and healing. For this to be realized, we must face each conflict with courage and confidence, knowing that we can grow from every difficult situation.

Developing skills in EQ is not an easy process because it requires us to both confront our inner self while changing our external interactions. In many ways, we can be as much a mystery to ourselves as God is a mystery to us. Our growth is fueled, in part, by living through profoundly challenging interpersonal and group experiences. It is the pain within those encounters that can motivate us to improve ourselves and change our behavior with others. It is essential for religious leaders to be in continual growth—the importance of this process cannot be overstated. We have provided many tools in previous chapters that can assist you on this journey.

You have chosen to re-create yourself in astonishing ways by becoming an emotionally intelligent religious leader. With your newfound wisdom and skill, you have the power to transform your leadership and the positive effect you have in your ministry. May God bless you in your service to others.

NOTES

I. INTRODUCTION

1. Andrew Coleman, *A Dictionary of Psychology*, third edition (Oxford: Oxford University Press, 2008).

2. N. G. Naidu, "Emotional Intelligence in Leadership," *International Journal of Entrepreneurship and Business Environment Perspectives* 3, no. 1 (2012): 727–30.

3. B. Wall, "Being Smart Only Takes You So Far," *Training and Development* 61, no. 1 (2007): 64–65.

4. Daniel Goleman, *Emotional Intelligence: Why It Can Matter More Than IQ* (New York: Bantam Books, 1995).

5. J. L. Spencer, B. E. Winston, and M. C. Bocarnea, "Predicting the Level of Pastors' Risk of Termination/Exit from the Church," *Pastoral Psychology* 61, no. 1 (2012): 85–98.

6. Wayne Cordeiro, *Leading on Empty: Refilling Your Tank and Renewing Your Passion* (Minneapolis, MN: Bethany House, 2010), 48–49.

7. B. F. Batool, "Emotional Intelligence and Effective Leadership," *Journal of Business Studies Quarterly* 4, no. 3 (2013): 84–94.

8. R. E. Boyatzis, T. Brizz, and L. N. Godwin, "The Effect of Religious Leaders' Emotional and Social Competencies on Improving Parish Vibrancy," *Journal of Leadership and Organizational Studies* 18, no. 2 (2011): 192–206, https://doi.org/10.1177/1548051810369676.

9. Martin Buber, *I and Thou*, trans. Walter Kaufmann (New York: Charles Scribner's Sons, 1970), 57.

10. Roy M. Oswald, "Emotional Intelligence and Congregational Leadership," *Reflective Practice: Formation and Supervision in Ministry* 36 (2016): 102.

11. Roy Oswald and Arland Jacobson, *The Emotional Intelligence of Jesus* (Lanham, MD: Rowman and[stet ampersands throughout] Littlefield, 2015), 136.

12. Larry Crabb, *Understanding Who You Are: What Your Relationships Tell You about Yourself* (Colorado Springs, CO: NavPress, 1997), 24–25.

13. R. W. Lamothe, "Types of Faith and Emotional Intelligence," *Pastoral Psychology* 59, no. 3 (2010): 331–44, http://dx.doi.org/10.1007/s11089-009-0229-3.

14. Roy M. Oswald, "Emotional Intelligence and Congregational Leadership," *Reflective Practice: Formation and Supervision in Ministry* 36 (2016): 109.

15. John Lee West, "An Analysis of Emotional Intelligence Training and Pastoral Job Satisfaction," *Journal of Pastoral Care and Counseling* 70, no. 4 (2016): 228–43.

16. Daniel Goleman, Richard Boyatzis, and Annie McKee, *Primal Leadership: Learning to Lead with Emotional Intelligence* (Boston, MA: Harvard Business Press, 2013), 79–161.

2. EMOTIONAL SELF-AWARENESS
AS A FOUNDATION

1. Richard Rohr, *Things Hidden: Scripture as Spirituality* (Cincinnati, OH: Franciscan Media, 2008), 75–76.

2. Daniel Goleman, Richard Boyatzis, and Annie McKee, *Primal Leadership: Learning to Lead with Emotional Intelligence* (Boston: Harvard Business Press, 2013).

3. Roy Oswald and Arland Jacobson, *The Emotional Intelligence of Jesus* (Lanham, MD: Rowman and Littlefield, 2015).

4. Sun Tzu, *The Art of War* (Boulder, CO: Shambhala Publications, 2005).

5. Brenda Cooper, *Magical Realism in West African Fiction* (London: Routledge, 2012).

6. Goleman, Boyatzis, and McKee, *Primal Leadership: Learning to Lead with Emotional Intelligence*, 39.

7. D. Prime and A. Begg, *On Being a Pastor: Understanding Our Calling and Work* (Chicago: Moody Publishers, 2006), 18–22.

8. Elisabeth Elliott, *Through Gates of Splendor: The Event that Shocked the World, Changed a People, and Inspired a Nation* (Peabody, MA: Hendrickson Publishers, 2010), 17.

9. H. B. London and N. B. Wiseman, *Pastors at Greater Risk* (Ventura, CA: Gospel Light Publications, 2003), 2–52.

10. "The Incredibles," IMDb, http://www.imdb.com/title/tt0317705/quotes (accessed September 10, 2017).

11. G. L. McIntosh and D. Samuel Sr., *Overcoming the Dark Side of Leadership: The Paradox of Personal Dysfunction* (Grand Rapids, MI: Baker Books, 2007), 25–80.

12. F. N. Watts, R. Nye, and S. B. Savage, *Psychology for Christian Ministry* (London: Psychology Press, 2002), 296–97.

13. Richard Rohr, Center for Action and Contemplation, https://cac.org/ego-the-actor-2016-07-12/ (accessed September 11, 2017).

14. S. Horvath and C. C. Morf, "Narcissistic Defensiveness: Hypervigilance and Avoidance of Worthlessness," *Journal of Experimental Social Psychology* 45, no. 6 (2009): 1252–58.

15. Richard Rohr, *Things Hidden: Scripture as Spirituality* (Cincinnati, OH: Franciscan Media, 2008).

16. Movie Quotes and More, http://www.moviequotesandmore.com/creed-best-movie-quotes/ (accessed October 1, 2017).

17. Thomas Merton quote, https://www.goodreads.com/quotes/351865-pride-makes-us-artificial-humility-makes-us-real (accessed September 23, 2017).

18. Gautama Buddha, *The Dhammapada: The Buddha's Path of Wisdom*, trans. Acharya Buddharakkhita (Lismore, Australia: Dharma Education Association Inc., 1998).

19. N. Pembroke, "Pastoral Care or Shame-based Perfectionism?" *Pastoral Psychology* 61, no. 2 (2012): 245–58.

20. John Eldredge, *Wild at Heart: Discovering the Secret of a Man's Soul* (New York: Harper Collins, 2011), 149.

21. Jonathan Kellerman, *Over the Edge* (New York: Ballantine Books, 1987), 40.

22. John Lee West, "An Analysis of Emotional Intelligence Training and Pastoral Job Satisfaction," *Journal of Pastoral Care and Counseling* 70, no. 4 (2016): 228–43.

23. Robert McCammon, *Freedom of the Mask* (Burton, MI: Subterranean Press, 2015), 55.

24. David G. Benner, "Perfection and the Harmonics of Wholeness," "Perfection," *Oneing*, 4, no. 1 (CAC: 2016): 61–63. This article was adapted from David G. Benner, *Human Being and Becoming* (Ada, MI: Brazos Press, 2016).

25. Donald Miller, *Blue Like Jazz* (Nashville: Thomas Nelson, 2003), 220.

26. R. A. Johnson, *Owning Your Own Shadow: Understanding the Dark Side of the Psyche* (New York: Harper Collins, 2013), 12–68.

27. Troy Denning, *The Sorcerer: Return of the Archwizards* (New York: Holtzbrinck Publishers, 2002).

28. Carl G. Jung, *The Integration of the Personality* (New York: Farrar and Rinehart, 1939).

29. Lisa Fantino, *Shrouded in Pompei* (Mamaroneck, NY: Wanderlust Women Travel Ltd., 2014), 55.

30. John Lee West, "An Analysis of Emotional Intelligence Training and Pastoral Job Satisfaction," PhD diss., University of Colorado, Colorado Springs, 2015, ProQuest (10108302), 65.

31. Richard Rohr, *Falling Upward: A Spirituality for the Two Halves of Life* (San Francisco: Jossey-Bass, 2011), 136.

3. DEVELOPING EMOTIONAL SELF-AWARENESS

1. Don Riso and Hudson Russ, *The Wisdom of the Enneagram: the Complete Guide to Psychological and Spiritual Growth for the Nine Personality Types* (New York: Bantam Books,1999), 9.

2. Richard Rohr, "The Enneagram: The Discernment of Spirits," video workshop (Albuquerque, NM: Center for Action and Contemplation, 2004). The video is available on the Center for Action and Contemplation website's bookstore, http://store.cac.org.

3. Jim Manney, "Kataphatic or Apophatic Prayer?" IgnatianSpirituality.com, https://www.ignatianspirituality.com/2026/kataphatic-or-apophatic-prayer (accessed September 23, 2017).

4. Cynthia Bourgeault, *The Heart of Centering Prayer: Nondual Christianity in Theory and Practice* (Boulder, CO: Shambhala Publications, 2016), 23.

5. "The Twelve Steps of Alcoholics Anonymous," aa.org, http://www.aa.org/assets/en_US/smf-121_en.pdf.

6. Bob Smith and Bill Wilson, *The Big Book: Alcoholics Anonymous*, fourth edition (New York: Alcoholics Anonymous World Services, Inc., 2001).

7. J. P. Kremenitzer, "The Emotionally Intelligent Early Childhood Educator: Self-reflective Journaling," *Early Childhood Education Journal* 33, no. 1 (2005): 3–9.

8. Gloria Wilcox, "The Feeling Wheel: A Tool for Expanding Awareness of Emotions and Increasing Spontaneity and Intimacy," *Transactional Analysis*

Journal 12, no. 4 (1982): 274–76, https://doi.org/10.1177/ 036215378201200411.

9. Gautama Buddha, *The Dhammapada: The Buddha's Path of Wisdom*, trans. Acharya Buddharakkhita (Lismore, Australia: Dharma Education Association, Inc., 1998).

10. Joseph Luft and Harrington Ingham, "The Johari Window, A Graphic Model of Interpersonal Awareness," Proceedings of the Western Training Laboratory in Group Development (Los Angeles: University of California Press, 1955).

11. William Hutchinson, "Ministry Matters," http://www.ministrymatters. com/all/entry/6843/what-is-spiritual-direction (accessed September 1, 2017).

12. J. R. Ragsdale, C. Orme-Rogers, J. C. Bush, S. L. Stowman, and R. W. Seeger, "Behavioral Outcomes of Supervisory Education in the Association for Clinical Pastoral Education: A Qualitative Research Study," *Journal of Pastoral Care and Counseling* 70, no.1, (2016): 5–15.

13. Association for Clinical Pastoral Education, https://www.acpe.edu/ ACPE/_Students/FAQ_S.aspx (accessed September 15, 2017).

14. Scott Thomas and Tom Wood, *Gospel Coach: Shepherding Leaders to Glorify God* (Grand Rapids, MI: Zondervan, 2012), 23–62.

15. Carl G. Jung, *Letters of C. G. Jung: Volume I, 1906–1950* (London: Routledge, 2015), 33.

4. UTILIZING EMOTIONAL SELF-CONTROL

1. Steven King, *The Waste Lands* (New York: Signet Books, 1991), 18.

2. Adele B. Lynn, *The EQ Interview* (New York: AMACOM Books, 2008), 9.

3. *Tesla Life and Legacy*, https://www.pbs.org/tesla/ll/ll_niagara.html (accessed October 1, 2017).

4. Charles Stone, "5 Scientifically Proven Mindfulness Skills that WILL Make You a Better Leader (and a Better Person)," Stonewell Ministries, http:// charlesstone.com/5-scientifically-proven-skills-that-make-you-a-better-leader/ (accessed October 3, 2017).

5. Daniel Goleman, *Working with Emotional Intelligence* (New York: Bantam, 1998).

6. Karen Friedman, *Shut Up and Say Something: Business Strategies to Overcome Strategies and Influence Listeners* (Santa Barbara, CA: ABC-CLIO Publishing, 2010), 73–74.

7. Harris Wittels, *Humblebrag: The Art of False Modesty* (New York: Grand Central Publishing, 2012).

8. Paul Stevens, *Where Do Pastors Go to Cry? Practical Principles You Won't Learn in Seminary* (Bloomington, IN: Anchor House, 2012), 62.

9. Nathan DeWall. "Self-control: Teaching Students About Their Greatest Inner Strength," American Psychological Association, http://www.apa.org/ed/precollege/ptn/2014/12/self-control.aspx (accessed September 15, 2017).

10. Jane Austen quote, https://www.goodreads.com/quotes/283094-i-will-be-calm-i-will-be-mistress-of-myself (accessed October 13, 2017).

11. Bohdi Sanders, "Warrior Wisdom: Ageless Wisdom for the Modern Warrior," Goodreads, https://www.goodreads.com/quotes/502832-never-respond-to-an-angry-person-with-a-fiery-comeback (accessed October 15, 2017).

5. GAINING EMPATHY

1. Walt Whitman, "The Song of Myself," *Leaves of Grass* (Brooklyn, NY, 1855).

2. Daniel Goleman, *Emotional Intelligence: Why It Can Matter More Than IQ* (New York: Bantam Books, 1995).

3. Audrey Hepburn quote, https://wnq-movies.com/post/143841592742/celebrating-audrey-hepburns-birthday-with-her-20 (accessed September 22, 2017).

4. Daniel Goleman, Richard E. Boyatzis, and Annie McKee, *Primal Leadership: Learning to Lead with Emotional Intelligence* (Boston: Harvard Business School Press, 2002), 3–4.

5. Homer quote, https://www.brainyquote.com/quotes/homer_153603 (accessed September 18, 2017)

6. Larry Crabb, *Understanding Who You Are: What Your Relationships Tell You about Yourself* (Colorado Springs, CO: NavPress, 1997).

7. 7. Mark B. Baer, "Empathy Can Lead to Profound Insights," *Psychology Today*, https://www.psychologytoday.com/blog/empathy-and-relationships/201612/empathy-can-lead-profound-insights (accessed November 15, 2017).

8. Marcus Aurelius quote, https://www.goodreads.com/quotes/685844-whenever-you-are-about-to-find-fault-with-someone-ask (accessed September 14, 2017).

9. M. Scott Peck quote, http://www.azquotes.com/quote/816324 (accessed October 30, 2017).

10. Ron Cook, "Who Is Caring for Superman?" *Care for Pastors*, http://careforpastors.org/who-is-caring-for-superman/ (accessed October 3, 2017).

11. Ibid.

12. Scott Thomas and Tom Wood, *Gospel Coach: Shepherding Leaders to Glorify God* (Grand Rapids, MI: Zondervan, 2012), 23–62.

13. Matthew Fox, *A Spirituality Named Compassion* (San Francisco: Harper and Row, 1990), 88.

6. LEARNING ORGANIZATIONAL AWARENESS

1. Henry Mintzberg, *Mintzberg on Management: Inside Our Strange World of Organizations* (New York: Simon and Schuster, 1989).

2. Daniel Goleman, Richard E. Boyatzis, Vanessa Druskat, and Michele Nevarez, *Organizational Awareness: A Primer* (Florence, MA: More Than Sound, 2017), 3.

3. Lawrence E. Susskind, Sarah McKearnen, and Jennifer Thomas-Lamar, eds., *The Consensus Building Handbook: A Comprehensive Guide to Reaching Agreement*, (Thousand Oaks, CA: Sage, 1999), 108.

4. Nadyne Guzmán. "The Leadership Covenant: Essential Factors for Developing Cocreative Relationships within a Learning Community," *The Journal of Leadership Studies* 2, no. 4 (1995): 151–60.

5. Gary McIntosh and Charles Arn, *What Every Pastor Should Know: 101 Indispensable Rules for Leading Your Church* (Grand Rapids, MI: Baker Books, 2013).

6. Harold Dwight Lasswell, *Politics: Who Gets What, When, and How* (New York: Whittlesey House, 1936).

7. Richard S. Sharf, *Theories of Psychotherapy and Counseling*, third edition (Boston: Cengage, 2015).

7. ESTABLISHING INFLUENCE

1. Stephen R. Covey, *The 7 Habits of Highly Effective People: Powerful Lessons in Personal Change* (New York: Free Press, 2004), 10.

2. Daniel Goleman, Richard E. Boyatzis, and Annie McKee, *Primal Leadership: Learning to Lead with Emotional Intelligence* (Boston: Harvard Business School Press, 2002), 40.

3. John L. West, "An Analysis of Emotional Intelligence Training and Pastoral Job Satisfaction," PhD diss., University of Colorado, Colorado Springs, 2015, ProQuest (10108302), 75.

4. Reuven Bar-On, "The Bar-On Model of Emotional-Social Intelligence (ESI)," http://www.eiconsortium.org/pdf/baron_model_of_emotional_social_intelligence.pdf (accessed November 19, 2017).

5. Lou Gerstner quote, https://www.supanet.com/find/famous-quotes-by/lou-gerstner/its-about-communication-fqb10294/ (accessed November 19, 2017).

6. Donald Miller, *Blue Like Jazz* (Nashville: Thomas Nelson, Inc., 2003), 220.

7. Richard S. Sharf, *Theories of Psychotherapy and Counseling*, third edition (Boston: Cengage, 2015).

8. Henry Cloud and John Townsend, *How to Have That Difficult Conversation You've Been Avoiding* (Grand Rapids, MI: Zondervan, 2005).

9. Pamela Spahr, "What Is Transformational Leadership? How New Ideas Produce Impressive Results," St. Thomas University Online, https://online.stu.edu/transformational-leadership/ (accessed November 20, 2017).

10. Benjamin Hoff, *The Tao of Pooh* (London: Penguin Group, 1982), 40.

11. Lawrence E. Susskind, Sarah McKearnen, and Jennifer Thomas-Lamar, *The Consensus Building Handbook: A Comprehensive Guide to Reaching Agreement* (Thousand Oaks, CA: Sage Publications, 1999).

12. West, "An Analysis of Emotional Intelligence Training and Pastoral Job Satisfaction," 72.

8. EMBRACING CONFLICT MANAGEMENT

1. Catrienne McGuire, *Cry Silently Pray Loudly* (London: Austin Macauley, 2016).

2. Maya Angelou quote, https://www.brainyquote.com/quotes/maya_angelou_392897 (accessed November 15, 2017).

3. Kenneth Boa, "Conflict Management," Bible.org, https://bible.org/seriespage/19-conflict-management (accessed November 15, 2017).

4. Klute Blackson, "Positively Positive," http://www.positivelypositive.com/2013/10/27/what-other-people-think-about-you-is-none-of-your-business (accessed November 15, 2017).

5. Malachy McCourt quote, https://www.brainyquote.com/quotes/malachy_mccourt_307621 (accessed November 15, 2017).

6. Donald Miller, *Blue Like Jazz* (Nashville: Thomas Nelson, 2003), 221.

7. John L. West, "An Analysis of Emotional Intelligence Training and Pastoral Job Satisfaction" PhD diss., University of Colorado, Colorado Springs, 2015, ProQuest (10108302), 80.

8. Ibid.

9. Finley Peter Dunne, "Comforting the Afflicted and Afflicting the Comfortable," Shawn Thomas blog, https://shawnethomas.com/2012/09/16/comforting-the-afflicted-afflicting-the-comfortable-james-19-11/ (accessed November 18, 2017).

10. Thomas Paine quote, https://www.goodreads.com/quotes/350557-the-harder-the-conflict-the-more-glorious-the-triumph-what (accessed November 19, 2017).

9. SPIRITUALITY OF THE EMOTIONALLY INTELLIGENT RELIGIOUS LEADER

1. Henri J. M. Nouwen, *Making All Things New: An Invitation to the Spiritual Life* (New York: HarperCollins, 1981), 21.

2. Richard Rohr, *Falling Upward: A Spirituality for the Two Halves of Life* (San Francisco: Jossey-Bass, 2011), 158.

3. Pope Francis, *The Joy of the Gospel* (Erlanger, KY: The Dynamic Catholic Institute), 198–99.

4. Peter Scazzero, *Emotionally Healthy Spirituality: It's Impossible to be Spiritually Mature While Remaining Emotionally Immature* (Grand Rapids, MI, 2006), 15.

5. Wayne Teasdale, *The Mystic Heart: Discovering a Universal Spirituality in the World's Religions* (Novato, CA: New Word Library, 1999), 17.

10. CONCLUSION

1. Dale Carnegie, *How to Win Friends and Influence People* (New York: Simon and Schuster, 2010).